COWBOY HIGH STYLE

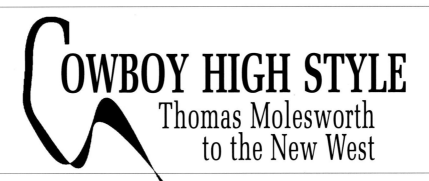

COWBOY HIGH STYLE
Thomas Molesworth
to the New West

Elizabeth Clair Flood

GIBBS·SMITH
P
PUBLISHER

PEREGRINE SMITH BOOKS

SALT LAKE CITY

First paperback edition
97 96 95   5 4 3 2 1

Text copyright © 1992 by Elizabeth Clair Flood
Photograph copyrights as noted

This is a Peregrine Smith Book, published by
Gibbs Smith, Publisher
P.O. Box 667
Layton, UT 84041

Designed by Mary Ellen Thompson
Line art throughout this book is by Frederic Remington
from various issues of *Century Magazine*
Manufactured by Times Publishing Group, Singapore

Library of Congress Cataloging-in-Publication Data

Flood, Elizabeth Clair, 1967-
Cowboy high style : Thomas Molesworth to the new west
/ Elizabeth Clair Flood.
p. cm.
ISBN 0-87905-672-x (pbk.)
1. Furniture—West (U.S.) 2. Decoration and ornament,
Rural—West (U.S.)   3. Interior decoration—United
States—History-20th century.   I. Title.
NK2423.F57 1992
747.218'09'045—dc20   92-13938
                                    CIP

FOR MOM AND DAD
AND MY COACH TIM

CONTENTS

ACKNOWLEDGMENTS   9

INTRODUCTION   11

CREATING THE DREAM   27

REVIVAL   53

GALLERY OF FURNITURE
        AND ACCESSORIES   91

MIXING STYLES   137

JUST A TOUCH OF COWBOY   151

SOURCES   169

ACKNOWLEDGMENTS

I would never have pulled off this project or had so much fun if it weren't for the enthusiasm and contributions of a slew of cowboy-crazy people.

Thanks to my many hosts in Cody, Wyoming: Jimmy, Lynda and Alice Covert; Ken and Jill Siggins; Mike and Virginia Patrick; Castle Rock; Bryan, Marc and Adele Taggart; and, of course, the head honcho, Lloyd Taggart, whose love of Thomas Molesworth and his furniture was happily contagious. Thanks to the Buffalo Bill Museum, which provided me with extensive research material on Thomas Molesworth and his work. For their participation at a special gathering of former Molesworth employees and contemporary furniture makers, hosted by the Taggarts, I must also thank Paul Hindman, Ruth Taggart Blair, Speed Spiegleberg, and Jesse Frost for helping me piece together Molesworth's career. Thomas Molesworth's children, Lee Molesworth and Jean Lambert, were also invaluable.

At home in Jackson I am grateful for Adam McCool's extraordinary patience and encouragement, Scott McKinley's enthusiasm and imagination, and Pat's props and weeds. Thanks also to Angus Thuermer, Jr., and Mike Sellett of the *Jackson Hole News* for my first writing job, and to Gibbs Smith, my publisher, and Madge Baird, my editor, for my first book.

Finally, an enormous cowboy hug to my two new friends, Sandy and Terry Winchell of Fighting Bear Antiques in Jackson Hole, without whose knowledge, energy, and love this project would never have spun out of the chute.

*P*art of living the cowboy romance is owning a cozy cabin in the woods. Lloyd Taggart is especially proud of his cowboy retreat, furnished with Thomas Molesworth originals, located in his backyard in Cody, Wyoming.

ᚼINTRODUCTION

In the northwest corner of Wyoming, brisk winds whistle over boundless plains of sagebrush and up through ancient citadels of red rock. Below the wind-carved horizon formed by the Absaroka Mountain range, the South Fork of the Shoshone River laps idly in the frosty air as snow spirals across this uncivilized land. In the midst of this unbridled wilderness in the mid-1800s, a lonely cowboy, alias a jack-of-all-trades, sits by his pot-bellied stove, building a piece of furniture out of lodge-pole pine, a bundle of willows, and a stack of driftwood. After a summer and fall of tough, strenuous work with the cattle, winter is the season to stay warm and create a home.

Fine wood was scarce, and tools were crude, so early western furniture was designed to function. With an ax, a drawknife and a saw, a cowboy made something to sit on, sleep on, and eat off of. Style was not a priority. Little did this cowboy know that he and the early settlers who peeled poles with a drawknife and built furniture out of necessity were also building a tradition whose products would capture the eye of future western romantics and, a century later, be desired by furniture lovers worldwide.

Photographs © 1992 by David Swift

Today western furniture makers and designers are enjoying a heyday that would amaze the early cowboys who first created the style. People from San Francisco to New York and around the world yearn to furnish their homes using lodgepole, swollen burls, antlers, cowhide, and western memorabilia. Furniture makers, designers, and collectors are bombarded with phone calls, and western artifacts have flooded the market.

Since old cowboy pieces are hard to find, many people are opting for reproductions and/or a contemporary western style. "There are a lot of western items being reproduced today," says Tyler Beard of True West, which collects western furniture and accessories for Ralph Lauren and other western aficionados. "The demand is so great this year that there is not enough old to go around." Beard predicts cowboy lamps will be sold at K Mart one day, to match the current southwestern look of blankets and pale-colored lamp shades.

The first person to fashion the functional cowboy-culture high style, and still the leading light of the western furniture and style movement, was Cody, Wyoming's

For the TE Ranch, Molesworth's genius for high style was demonstrated by the incorporation of "keyhole" chairs with blue seats. The keyhole shape is elegant and reflects impeccable craftsmanship. Throughout his career Molesworth continued to experiment with the basic shape of the keyhole chair, carving designs on a solid piece of wood, as these two show, or cutting away the wood to expose cowboy silhouettes corralled in the keyhole. ▲

▶ Molesworth incorporated Indian designs and bold colors into his furniture. To cover couch cushions, he used red Chimayo weavings, designed and made in Chimayo Indian settlements approximately thirty miles north of Santa Fe. Routed designs were also used in most of Molesworth's interiors. Photo © 1992 by David Swift

own Thomas Molesworth (1890–1977) known as Moley in his hometown. In his interiors Molesworth created a western fantasy with burls, bright leather, Chimayo weavings, Navajo blankets, western objects, Indian artifacts, and artwork like cowboy paintings by E. W. Gollings and Indian scenes by Joseph Henry Sharp. Some of Molesworth's important commissions included the Cody TE Ranch for Bob Woodruff, the Rockefeller Ranch in Jackson, Wyoming, and President Dwight Eisenhower's den in Gettysburg, Pennsylvania. He also furnished some of the largest hotels during his day, such as the Plains Hotel in Cheyenne, Wyoming, the Wort in Jackson, Wyoming, and the Northern in Billings, Montana.

Molesworth was the first designer savvy enough to know he could sell the western mystique and ambience to easterners for big bucks. His furniture and style transcended the West of Stetsons, chewing tobacco, and cattle drives. In an article in the Billings, Montana paper in 1946, the writer reported: "'Ah,' said Molesworth in effect. 'This is dude ranch country. The dudes are always screaming their appreciation of homemade furniture. Why wouldn't they buy such stuff if it measured up to their standards of beauty and comfort?'" And they did.

Across the country there has been a renaissance of Molesworth's work; pieces once stuffed in back rooms, taken for granted, or simply thrown away are now worth anywhere from five hundred to twenty-five thousand dollars. "We always had Molesworth furniture around," says

Jimmy Covert's small chest, called the Canyon Spirit Bachelor Chest, reflects the artist's intrigue with the West and appreciation of American Indian culture. The chest's design, inspired by petroglyphs Covert stumbled upon in Thermopolis, Wyoming, tells the story of an eagle's ascent to power. Covert collaborated on the design with his Blackfoot Oneida friend, Rodney Skenendore.

Photograph © 1992 by David Swift

sleek pair of pointy boots is cowboy chic.

(Photo by Scott McKinley, courtesy Flat Creek Saddle Shop)

a young resident who grew up in Cody on a ranch in the South Fork Valley. "We knew it was beautiful, but if we stopped living with the furniture, that would take the joy out of the place." Fighting Bear Antiques of Jackson Hole, Wyoming, has played a leading role in turning up Molesworth furniture and setting the prices.

Inspired by Molesworth, as well as the resurgent interest in the Old West, furniture makers are popping up from Montana to Arizona to Texas. Their work ranges from traditional ranch-style furniture to more stylized art pieces. Their furniture, made of driftwood, longhorn, or peeled pole, often emblazoned with silhouettes of cowboys, wildlife, and Indians, packages the romantic West.

The West is in. *Dances with Wolves* was the first western to win an Academy Award for best picture since *Cimarron* back in 1931; New York stockbrokers are wearing bolo ties and cowboy boots on Wall Street; Parisian models are swinging Chanel fringed denim skirts; dude ranches are experiencing an influx of city slickers; and art collectors are scouring the Rocky Mountains for silver spurs, Navajo jewelry, blankets, and Santa Fe oils.

Modern Americans seem mind-boggled by the high-speed pace of city life, the dizzying onslaught of new technology and the abundance of cheap imports. They crave a simpler lifestyle and a closeness with nature. The West and western memorabilia seem to represent an authentic America to them.

Prior to the 1900s there was little western furniture to speak of. Western settlers learned the hard way that transporting furniture was a difficult feat. Pioneers who traveled the Oregon Trail in the mid-1840s and fifties soon discovered that heirlooms that had seemed so precious in St. Louis were expendable. The first time a team of oxen floundered fording a river, iron stoves, dry sinks, oak bureaus and tables hit the rocky trail. Then, as the trail weaved its way into the high mountains, travelers were forced to toss out other family heirlooms, such as mirrors, rocking chairs, or a piano. By 1875 a veritable warehouse of secondhand furniture stretched across Wyoming.

When the pioneers arrived at their destinations—or went bust and stayed in Wyoming and Montana—the best way to get furniture was to make it. Early designs were basic. A table was built to feed a large and growing

Frederic Remington.

family. Living conditions for early cattle raisers were rough and house interiors sparse. There wasn't much time to decorate because they were busy tending the cattle and coping with the hazards of living in the Wild West.

With the coming of the railroads and the establishment of rural mail in the 1900s, the more affluent were able to order from catalogs such as Montgomery Ward and Sears and Roebuck. Sears and Roebuck had an overwhelming selection of furniture ranging from their thirty-four-cent chair and their finest twenty-four-dollar sideboard to the "most stylish suite" ever sold. Some early settlers couldn't bear the thought of anything rustic in their homes, so they acquired oak furniture from back East. Less affluent families had more practical uses for the catalogs in their outhouses.

Not only was furniture scarce, but delivery of goods into the wilderness was often almost impossible. One family in Jackson Hole ordered a piano from the East, but because it was so heavy, it couldn't be transported over Teton Pass. A special cart was rigged, and movers pulled Jackson Hole's first piano into the valley over an Indian trail at its north end.

As more people moved into the West at the turn of the century, the area was no longer considered a dangerous or difficult place to visit. Soon towns became civilized enough to make suitable outposts for tourists. With improved transportation and increased prosperity in America, more people turned west for their dream vacations. Many were tiring of their rustic Adirondack lodges, which had kept hunters and other adventurers amused since the 1870s. As the Adirondacks filled with people and homes, the once wilderness was transformed into a bustling society, and those who had originally

vacationed there wished to escape. Determined outdoorspeople, hunters, and nature lovers sought a new frontier.

Owen Wister's *The Virginian*, Frederic Remington's and Charlie Russell's illustrations, and the "penny dreadful" novels glamorizing the lives of Billy the Kid and Wild Bill Hickok helped spin a magical myth of the West which attracted eastern romantics and adventure seekers to the frontier. The open land and the possibilities for

Dudes enjoy playing cowboy for a day in front of a cabin at the White Grass Dude Ranch in Jackson Hole, circa 1919.

Photograph courtesy of the Teton County Historical Center

Ranch hands were often asked to build lodgepole furniture during the winter and furnish ranch houses and cabins for summer visitors. The interior of the White Grass Ranch highlights essential elements of a western room still used today: an animal mount over a fireplace, Navajo rugs, and indigenous wood.

hunting and exploring drew the travel-hungry west. The more the press embellished the West, the more men and women wanted to wear cowboy boots and overalls, and ride off into the sunset in a ten-gallon hat.

Cattlemen soon discovered people were a more profitable stock than cattle. Ranches became classy getaway spots for eastern travelers. Eastern tourists had a preconceived notion of what the West should be, and the early

dude ranch entrepreneurs set about making their ranches fit those images. Acting not on reality, but on an exaggerated, romantic notion, they invented the western interior style—comfortable, yet rustic. As Struthers Burt, one of Jackson's earliest dude ranchers in the 1920s and a former Princeton professor, wrote in his *Diary of a Dude Wrangler:* "If you wish to sum up the dude business in one sentence, it consists in giving people homemade bedsteads but 40 pound mattresses."

Dude ranchers like Burt were also instrumental in the development of the western style. Because they were often forced to fill an entire ranch house and guest cabins

The Bear Paw Ranch in Jackson Hole, was the Seaton homestead in 1928. It was later purchased by Coulter Huyler in 1926 and became a dude ranch. Today the ranch has been divided among private individuals. Only twenty acres, now called the Rocking H, remain in the Huyler family.

Wyoming dude ranches, like Struthers Burt's Bar BC, the second dude ranch in Jackson Hole, attracted wealthy easterners west, where grandiose mountains towered over wild fields of sage. Like other dude wranglers, Burt strove to make vacationers' stays rugged 'n' western without depriving them of civilized luxuries like fine mattresses. The first visitors to the Bar BC arrived by train, followed by wagon in 1919.

with furniture in a short amount of time, ranchers had to rely on natural resources and immediate labor. "Out of sagebrush and deadfall," Burt and a partner set about building a ranch with cabins for eastern visitors seeking a rugged, romantic, but luxurious vacation in the West.

Burt writes: "Such a task might seem impossible unless you bear in mind the astonishing short time it takes experts to build a log-house and the genius of the westerner for turning his hand to anything. Our fireplaces were built by a man who had never built a fireplace before in his life and the rocks with which he had to work were the worst that can be imagined—slippery cobblestones and unshaped granite. The same man who one day is laying logs, the next can manufacture the pleasantest kind of an easy chair or a dining room table."

Because traveling west was originally a luxury, dude ranchers catered to the wealthy. Howard Eaton, the first man to recognize the potential of dude ranching and the importance of the whole western experience, established a dude ranch in 1879 in North Dakota on the east side of the Little Missouri River. At first the Eaton brothers invited friends from the East as a natural gesture of hospitality. Because the Eatons were enchanting hosts and enthusiastic sportsmen, they enticed more people to the West. Soon they were taking paying guests such as Theodore Roosevelt hunting and on some of the first pack trips into Yellowstone. As one person said of Eaton, "His guest list read like the New York Social Register." Later many of these guests would return to the West to build their own homes and furnish them much the way they remembered their first dude ranch.

In 1903 the Eatons established a dude ranch in Wolf, Wyoming, in the shadow of the Big Horns, to be closer to

Yellowstone Park and in the midst of the historic West. Easterners enthralled with the idea of living in the West came out and helped the Eatons build up the place. Some of these guests then became permanent residents and ranch owners. "What began to develop here was a feeling of home generated in the same sense that people built cottages in Maine or the inland lakes, which they returned to year after year," wrote Bucky King, author of *The Dude Connection.*

At the Valley Ranch in Cody, Larry Larom from New York built his dude ranch on much of the same philosophy as the Eaton brothers. He knew that the dramatic scenery of South Fork Valley, the abundance of game and the charm of ranch living could attract a number of guests. He also knew that the look and feel of a ranch were important. He furnished his cabins with some Adirondack furniture he had brought from home in 1915 to make the experience more rustic and appealing to the eastern tourists. When these wore out, he had his ranch hands cover the chairs with rawhide. At this time other ranches used antlers, steer horns, and lodgepole to create a western feeling. In the Northwest a few moose-antler chairs and tables were designed, and Texas ranchers were renowned for chairs, tables, and coatracks made from longhorn steer horns. While the horn furniture was more of a novelty than a trend, visitors were immediately attracted to the look.

In 1904 the Old Faithful Inn opened in Yellowstone Park, attracting a wealthy crowd who were interested in seeing the wilderness but insistent on luxury and conveniences. The rustic refinement of the grand lodge and the unusual interior of gnarly pine, Arts and Crafts furniture, and colorful Indian rugs were the epitome of elegance at the time and a monument to the development of western high style.

When hunters and tourists came West in the early 1900s, the West looked like the West they imagined. From

Photograph © 1992 by David Swift

Photograph © 1992 by David Swift

Photo courtesy Buffalo Bill Historical Center, Cody, WY

hunting to campfires to drinking whiskey and sleeping in a lodgepole bed, the West was an idyllic place to vacation. Dude ranchers planted the seeds for a new rustic and fashionable style to develop in America, one that caught on because of a sense of necessity and later the influence of the eastern settler's imagination. While ranches and their furniture were still fairly crude at the turn of the century, the West awaited a catalyst who could capitalize on its elements and the rustic tradition and turn western style into high fashion.

*T*he early cowboy used materials he had on hand to make a piece of furniture. This crude chair, made of unpeeled pole and hide, sits on the porch of an old cabin at the Valley Ranch in Cody, Wyoming. While the chair, built circa 1911, looks worn, it has withstood the test of time bravely and is still a sturdy piece of furniture. ◄

◄ Horn furniture was popular in Texas at the turn of the century. While rooms were rarely furnished entirely in horn furniture, individual pieces were used as novelty items in ranch homes.

◄ This rustic armchair, made circa 1900 from peeled tree branches, is typical of the functional early cowboy furniture.

▶ Interior decor at Old Faithful Inn blended the rustic feeling of knotty pine with the luxury of chiffon curtains. Bottom right is the lobby at Old Faithful Inn. The inn was originally furnished in part by the Old Hickory Furniture Company, which still operates today in Shelbyville, Indiana.

Photograph courtesy of the National Park Service

Photo courtesy of the National Park Service

CREATING THE DREAM

Since pioneers trekked across the country in search of a fresh start, the West has been a romanticized place. Tales of cowboys and desperados reached the East, inspiring dreams of adventure and action for the rugged individualist. The love of gold and the coming of the railroad drew more people west, promising families and individuals wealth and a new beginning in the 1850s. In 1883 Buffalo Bill's Wild West Show traveled east, generating more western romance and intensifying the myth. Suddenly in 1890 artists like Frederic Remington were documenting the fading of the West. With romance and nostalgia in people's hearts, the West became less a place

27

of reality and more a realm of imagination.

One man had the brains and ingenuity to realize western design was grounded in this romantic image and bigger than the dude ranches that had invented it. If easterners would pay big money to come a great distance to sit in a rustic chair, it seemed logical that they would pay something to have a rustic chair of their own. This man was Thomas Canada Molesworth. Like Buffalo Bill, the Union Pacific, hotel owners and dude ranchers, he enjoyed perpetuating the romance of the West.

Molesworth was also serious about design and craftsmanship in much the same way as his contemporaries, Frank Lloyd Wright and Gustav Stickley. Like Wright, he was concerned with controlling all the elements of interior design. From leather walls to furniture to copper ashtrays, Molesworth created a complete western look.

Molesworth was concerned with the overall effect of a room rather than with the importance of one piece of furniture. This early roomscape from the Coe Lodge, circa 1940, illustrates important elements of a Molesworth interior, from a large iron fire screen to a magazine holder faced with half-poles.

A fireplace with an iron screen of animal silhouettes was often the focal point of a Molesworth room, as it is in this living room in the Pahaska Tepee Ski Lodge in Yellowstone National Park. This photo was taken at Christmas time before the lodge burned in 1942.

He was exposed to the elements of western furniture and to the components of the Arts and Crafts, Adirondack, and Art Deco furniture styles while studying at the Chicago Art Institute in 1908 and 1909, a time when Chicago was a major force in the world of modern decorative arts and furniture design. Molesworth also developed a sophisticated taste by traveling extensively, taking an interest in contemporary artists, and socializing with some of the most influential people of the time.

Born in Kansas in 1890 to a preacher, Molesworth grew up with his parents and three siblings. As a child he learned to ride horses and later developed an interest in art. After Molesworth's first year at the Chicago Art Institute, his father discouraged his painting career: "You'll never be a Charlie Russell. Come home and make a living," he said. Molesworth took his advice. He worked for a time in a Chicago furniture company and then was a U.S. Marine corporal in France during the First World War. Following the war, Molesworth worked at a bank in South Dakota, then managed the Rowe Furniture Company in Billings. He married LaVerne Johnston, a native of Byron, Illinois, in 1917.

In search of his own business, Molesworth moved his wife and two young children, Lee and Jean, to Cody, Wyoming, in 1931. "He said he would rather die broke than work for someone else," his son Lee would say later. There he opened the Shoshone Furniture Company on Sheridan Avenue; his company was one of the first furniture shops in the small town, with its population of two thousand, offering commercial lines. Then Molesworth started selling his own handmade furniture and supplied caskets for the deceased; in those days furniture makers often took charge of this duty. He also became a dealer in western art and artifacts.

Molesworth's business was modest at first. He sold primitive fir and cedar pole furniture and did small jobs

Photograph © 1992 by David Swift

for individuals in the area. In 1933, however, Pennsylvania publishing mogul Moses Annenberg commissioned Molesworth to furnish his western retreat—a ten-thousand-square-foot lodge on a seven-hundred-acre spread in Wyoming, just west of the South Dakota border—a job

which launched Molesworth's career as a furniture-maker and interior designer. Annenberg wanted a place to fish, relax, and entertain—a place similar to the Adirondack "shanties" furnished by local craftsmen in the late 1800s and early 1900s.

Molesworth built 245 pieces of furniture for Annenberg's hunting lodge and designed the entire interior, from coyote-head sconces with lights suspended from their jaws to wrought-iron fireplace screens. The main room of the lodge featured bright upholstered furniture and cabinets carved with figures, including a piece with a bobcat head as a decoration and the creature's paw as the cabinet pull. There were chandeliers and fire screens of wrought-iron western cutouts suggesting Indian villages. He made horsehide drapes with beadwork, scattered forty-two Navajo rugs throughout the lodge, and built a twenty-foot table, accompanied by twenty high-backed chairs which were marked with the routed design of the letter *A* and had arms made of

Molesworth built his furniture to last. A Valley Ranch cabin, built in 1911, is furnished in original Molesworth, including the couch, table, and an unusual scalloped and skirted armchair. In order to spruce up the Molesworth furniture, the present owners reupholstered the couch and chair and added a floor lamp by contemporary furniture maker Ken Siggins. The room also features two Adirondack chairs, which were later covered in cowhide by Larry Larom, the original owner of the Valley Ranch.

burl. Molesworth also installed a bar routed with western motifs, and on a balcony, he placed Adirondack lounges. (Much of this furniture is now in the Buffalo Bill Museum or still at the Annenberg Lodge.)

Because Molesworth's furniture for Annenberg was rustic, all hand-peeled fir, a style was born, one hewn from the landscape. Later Molesworth would perfect this style and make it more cosmopolitan. For the Annenberg project, Molesworth hired a crew of six, and afterwards opened a shop and a log cabin on the corner of Sheridan Avenue. He usually worked steadily all day.

Some of Molesworth's most famous commissions were for hotels in Wyoming and Montana. When the Grand Hotel opened in 1886, it was one of the most sophisticated hotels in the wilderness. Molesworth remodeled the Grand about 1936. The hotel, which was later called the General Custer, closed in 1977.

A *Zia pot, nestled in an iron stand topped off with a bell-shaped sheepskin shade, was just one of the ways Molesworth incorporated Indian artifacts into a room. He also embellished his work with Indian designs for effect; for instance, note the use of the thunderbird image on this 1933-34 chair from the Northern Hotel in Billings, Montana, and the water serpent on the lamp shade.*

Evenings he often spent at the Directors Club in the Green Front, an old building just off Cody's main street, playing gin rummy with his buddies, or poker if it was Thursday.

Molesworth's immediate success was probably due to his aggressive skills as a self-promoter. Following the Annenberg project, he was commissioned to build furniture for big Wyoming and Montana hotels. These hotels needed a large amount of furniture and could afford to pay Molesworth's prices. In the early thirties he sold furniture to three Wyoming hotels: the Noble Hotel in Lander, the Plains Hotel in Cheyenne, and the Washakie

Photograph © 1992 by David Swift, courtesy of Fighting Bear Antiques

Hotel in Worland. He also designed one lobby of the Grand Hotel in Billings, Montana. Whether a conscious marketing technique on his part or not, hotels were a brilliant showcase for Molesworth's furniture, since wealthy customers were apt to visit these posh resorts and ask about the leather furniture made out of extraordinary burls. During this same era Molesworth decorated several other grand lodges and hotels, including the Sumer Lodge in Glenwood Springs, Colorado, later owned by Laura Hunt; the Northern Hotel in Billings, Montana; the Pendleton Hotel in Pendleton, Oregon; the Stockman's Hotel in Elko, Nevada; the Ferris Hotel in Rawlins, Wyoming; and the Simon Snyder Ranch on the North Fork near Cody.

About this time in western history, many affluent families were purchasing ranches in the West after spending time at a dude ranch or hunting camp. Molesworth gained entrance to this society through an elite hunting crowd he met in Cody. He was good friends with Cody hunting guide Max Wilde, Coca-Cola magnate Bob Woodruff, Chevrolet dealer Bud Webster, Husky Oil owner Glen Nielson, Wyoming Governor and Senator Millward Simpson, W.R. Coe of the Virginia Railroad, Louise Taggart and rancher-contractor Lloyd Taggart, Sr.—all of whom purchased his furniture.

Photo courtesy of Buffalo Bill Historical Center, Cody, WY, private collection

Molesworth also spent several vacations at Itchaway, Woodruff's plantation in Baker County, Georgia, hunting with his Cody gang and other important people such as John Olin and Richard Mellon. Other clients in the thirties included Tom Yawkey, owner of the Boston Red Sox, and Mickey Cochrane, a catcher for Detroit in the American League.

Neatly dressed in a vest and bolo tie, Molesworth fit right in with this affluent crowd. Everyone liked to have him around. He had a good sense of humor, played a serious game of gin rummy, spoke about art intelligently and was a good shot for quail and dove.

While Molesworth wasn't impressed with money, according to his children, he did cater to the wealthy. He considered individuals who walked into his showroom casual browsers and not worth his time. Ruth Taggart Blair says she was in charge of sorting out the people who came in according to money and taste. She admits this was a difficult task because some of the wealthiest people were dressed in jeans and a T-shirt. Molesworth, however, was pragmatic and didn't want to deal with browsers; he wanted to deal with people who were interested. Several of his friends have said that if he didn't know you, he could be perfectly cold.

During this time of socializing with powerful men,

The dining room of the TE Ranch is furnished with Molesworth's keyhole chairs and matching sideboards covered in bright blue leather.

Molesworth gained significant marketing coup by being invited to place his furniture in the front display window of Abercrombie and Fitch on Fifth Avenue in New York City. Sterling "Speed" Spiegleberg, who worked for Molesworth from 1935 to 1940, says he remembers seeing a New York newspaper clipping of the display, with a mob of curious observers pushed up against the window to see the western furniture and interior design. The fancy display window featured mannequins dressed in western attire, furniture, and a dollhouse-sized room decorated with furniture and accessories.

It took Molesworth only five years to be recognized by the New York elite as the first and only high-style western designer. Spiegleberg remembers this era—Molesworth's heyday—as one of many late nights, spent crating loads of furniture. The furniture was sold before it was made, and once it was made, it was shipped.

Although Molesworth was an effective businessman, he was also a true artist with a genius for design and quality. His furniture was made of fir because of the wood's strength and exotic grain, and his design shapes suggested modern contours and fashions. His materials were first-rate, he embraced Indian artifacts, and he incorporated the artwork of his contemporaries into his roomscapes. Also he was never afraid to have fun with a room. "It was those surprises he did that were so neat. He had so many ideas," says Ruth Taggart Blair, a Molesworth employee.

Molesworth touched a soft spot in people's hearts with his western furniture. It was sturdy yet whimsical, stylish yet functional, cosmopolitan yet romantic. Few questioned his taste because his stern and charming demeanor convinced his clients of his authority. If he thought a certain piece of furniture or a Charlie Russell sculpture would top off a room, he had no qualms about putting the

Photograph © 1992 by David Swift

Two display cases of Molesworth's personal collection of Indian artifacts are featured in the John Taggart Hinckley Library in Powell, Wyoming. This window features a parfleche, arrows, an eagle-feather bonnet with a beaded brow and ermine tails, a beaded pipe bag, a kachina doll, a medicine bundle, a possibles bag, and other Indian items. Molesworth was one of the first designers to use American Indian artifacts as decoratives in a room setting.

item on the bill. "And he got away with it," Ruth remembers.

"Tom believed in his work and if he liked you, he would do anything for you," she says. "He would even sell the paintings off his own wall." Jean Lambert, Molesworth's daughter, remembers her mother wondering whether their family would have anything to sit on in their own home. "He used to sell the furniture out from under us," Lambert says.

In 1940 Molesworth worked with Mrs. Nell Woodruff, the wife of Coca-Cola executive Bob Woodruff, to create one of his most sophisticated commissions, the TE Ranch, formerly Buffalo Bill's ranch. Molesworth decorated this home with his leather-upholstered furniture, suede curtains embellished with bead- work, an intricate woven rug, and many unique accessories such as his slender iron-rabbit ash tray, a lodgepole magazine rack with two beadwork pouches, and lamp pulls made from gun shells. He also purchased sand paintings made by Navajo Indians. Today these original sand paintings are virtually priceless. Besides the Indian artifacts, Molesworth relied on the artistic innovations of contemporary artists to create the ambience he wanted. He incorporated the handiwork of local and regional woodworkers, upholsterers, ironworkers, lampshade decorators and artists. Molesworth particularly respected the work of his Chicago classmate Edward Grigware, who painted a variety of murals and designed

Photograph © 1992 by David Swift

A one-of-a-kind piece, this hand-peeled pole credenza is decorated with a Southwest-inspired sun design and horn pulls. The four plinth blocks on the corners illustrate Molesworth's sophisticated sense of balance and style. ◀

Molesworth created a myriad of lamps to complement his western roomscapes. His silhouette lampshades, created by Cody craftsman Russell Blood, illustrate Molesworth's intrigue with the two-dimensional shape. The animal cutouts against parchment paper recreate the cozy outdoors feeling of a campfire. ▶

Photograph © 1992 by David Swift

the original gunfighter image– an image Molesworth used in numerous designs during his career, including on tables and a door at the Sumer Lodge, and later on chairs and a door at the TE Ranch.

Molesworth's most unusual collaborations with Grigware were his dioramas of people's homes. Molesworth used these lilliputian rooms to show clients what their houses would look like when he was done. Each miniature was carefully constructed and accurately painted. The rooms feature tiny Navajo blankets, lamps, and figures. One of his miniature roomscapes is on ex-

This iron door at Laura Hunt's lodge in Glenwood, Colorado, is reminiscent of the sharp and simple shapes of the Art Deco style. ◄

Molesworth wasn't afraid to embellish a western interior. With an eye for whimsy, he collaborated with Edward Grigware and inserted this diorama of an Indian village into a cupboard. ▶

hibit at the LDS Church in Cody.

The dioramas were also used for other commercial endeavors. Northwest Airlines commissioned Molesworth to design western dioramas for their home offices. The airlines also shipped these particular dioramas to travel shows across the country to generate interest in western vacations.

And finally, Molesworth and Grigware created dioramas purely for decoration. Molesworth once had Grigware construct a diorama of an American Indian village at the base of snowcapped mountains inside a cupboard.

Molesworth also incorporated the paintings of popular western artists of the time, such as Frank Tenney Johnson, J. H. Sharp, Winold Reiss, W. R. Leigh, Olaf

Wieghorst, and Olaf Seltzer, and woodcarvings by Marshall Wallace into his interior design. The work of these masters reflected Molesworth's good taste and showed off the artistic talent of the region.

In his shop Molesworth capitalized and relied on quality craftspeople. Doug Skilicorn, a fine upholsterer and technician, and a former employee of the Rowe Furniture Company, was Molesworth's right-hand man. Paul Hindman worked under Skilicorn and was one of the top furniture makers. Later, Hindman opened the Wyoming Furniture Company and became, one of Molesworth's contemporaries. Today there is much discussion among collectors over whether a piece is Molesworth's or Hindman's. Hindman was extremely prolific in creating Molesworth-style furniture when he worked on his own from 1938 to 1991.

Another exceptional employee was Speed Spiegleberg who worked in the shop at its pinnacle between 1935 and 1940. Russell Blood, an expert woodcarver, was originally hired to do mosaics with wood on furniture, but as this art was time consuming, Molesworth put him to work building furniture. Ruth Taggart Blair, with a degree in art from the Chicago Art Institute, helped design the rawhide lamp shades, curtains and rugs. Her most beautiful work is part of the TE collection. Other important employees included artist-builders George Dabich and Jesse Frost. After World War II Molesworth contracted with Cody woodworker Pete Fritjofson to make lathed poles which gave Molesworth's furniture a sleeker, more modern look.

While Molesworth was often difficult to work with, he valued his craftspeople and they respected his style. He was particularly a stickler about sanding and a perfectionist when it came to measurements and dimensions. Molesworth wanted his poles to look a certain way, and

*M*olesworth never seemed at a loss for a new idea. This carefully carved horse-head lamp base, made of walnut, was part of his private collection.

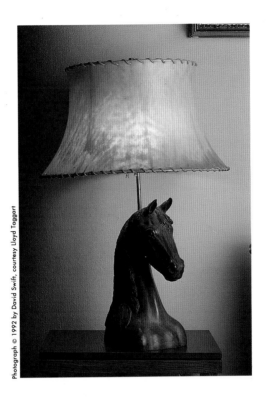

*M*olesworth designed this two-sided writing desk for use in the big hotels and dude ranches. The design is similar to Charles Limbert's Arts and Crafts desks of the early 1900s made for the Old Faithful Inn. In the latter half of Molesworth's career, he started using the lathed pole instead of hand carving each pole. This created a sleeker look for his 1950s clientele.

sandpaper with a specific friction had to be used. "He would have you peel the wood, then sand with coarse sandpaper, then finer sandpaper, then finer sandpaper," Spiegleberg says. He remembers that Molesworth always had something to say about the work in the shop. "After a while he didn't criticize as much, but he would say, 'That leg looks good, but what about the other three?'"

Above all, Molesworth knew where to find the best materials money could buy. Although his furniture looked rustic, its lines and dimensions were state of the art. He used Chimayos, that he bought from Ortega's Chimayo Weavings near Santa Fe, and he ordered mountains of leather form Branchard Brothers and Lane in New Jersey; he purchased stretched rawhide lamps from Leonard Foss Studios of Oakland, California; and local outfitters, such as Mel Stonehouse, hauled burls, fir, and unusual woods from the mountains. Molesworth also traveled to the Chicago Furniture Mart and combed trading posts in the Southwest for inspiration and unusual items.

Although Molesworth was ultraconscious about style, he never neglected function. His furniture was meant to be comfortable, sturdy and practical, and his accessories, such as lighting fixtures—rawhide-tipi chandeliers and mica sconces—were first-rate. He built furniture to house radios and phonographs and included horizontal compartments in ottomans for magazine storage. He also designed elegant iron ashtrays in the shapes of rabbits or donkeys. He used innersprings in his cushions for comfort, and his club chairs are almost the exact dimensions of a number 332 Gustav Stickley Morris chair. He also sloped the back and bottom of a chair for comfort. All these elements made his work far superior to that of local craftspeople.

Throughout his thirty-year career, Molesworth remained an artist. He was proud of his profession and

didn't grovel at anyone's feet for a job or money; he believed in his art. He cared about artists, his wealthy hunting crowd and the Cody community. He was also president of the Cody Club, commissioner of the American Legion, and a member of the Cody Lions Club. He always laughed and was the "same person in every crowd he mingled with," comments his daughter Jean.

In the mid-forties Molesworth received a call from someone in Jackson Hole requesting him to build furniture for a ranch. Molesworth said abruptly, "I'm busy and I wouldn't come to Jackson even if Mr. Rockefeller wanted his home decorated." The lady on the phone answered: "But, sir, it is Mr. Rockefeller." Finally Molesworth did agree to the commission. Other commissions in Jackson included the Wort Hotel, The Brinkerhoff, and the Hunter Hereford Ranch. The Brinkerhoff, originally a private residence and later sold to Grand Teton National Park to be used as a special retreat for VIPs, is the only Molesworth commission in Jackson still intact. The rest of the furniture was burned or sold because people grew tired of it.

Molesworth's furniture was in demand for approximately twenty-five years. During this time he skillfully managed the business. The value and prices of the furniture were never widely known. Molesworth never hung a price tag from any of his work—or even signed any of it, and prices which are known today don't seem to indicate any sort of pattern or pricing method.

He was known to be particularly lenient with his friends. "Tom was blasé about cost," a good friend says. "He never had the heart to charge what his services were worth." Molesworth charged the friend a moderate sum in 1950 for a sitting room fashioned around three original Coca-Cola illustrations. The room included a four-seat davenport, a fancy office desk and chair, a coffee table,

Zachary K. Brinkerhoff, of Dallas, Texas, in the late 1940s commissioned Molesworth to design his cabin overlooking Jackson Lake in Grand Teton National Park. The red Chimayo weavings on the chair and couch cushions—a Molesworth signature design—were often complemented by solid-colored leather furniture, such as the green chairs, round table, and two-tiered coffee table. At the back of the room sits one of Molesworth's iron donkey ashtrays. The red club chair was a direct copy of an Arts and Crafts chair in both style and dimensions.

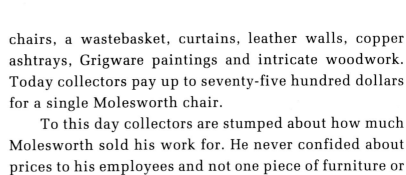

chairs, a wastebasket, curtains, leather walls, copper ashtrays, Grigware paintings and intricate woodwork. Today collectors pay up to seventy-five hundred dollars for a single Molesworth chair.

To this day collectors are stumped about how much Molesworth sold his work for. He never confided about prices to his employees and not one piece of furniture or accessory was marked. Although his prices must have been quite high for the time, he never wanted to sell something for more than what it was worth. In early 1974 he suggested a client sell his diorama for two thousand dollars. Many who knew Molesworth said it was his wife LaVerne who kept the finances in line while Tom continued to create.

In 1989 the Buffalo Bill Historical Center in Cody hosted a retrospective show, "Interior West, the Craft and Style of Thomas Molesworth." This exhibit in decorative arts was the museum's first in its sixty-five years of existence. Featuring individual pieces of furniture and a variety of roomscapes, the show was a grand success and served as a catalyst for the present rage for original Molesworth furniture. More people were exposed to the style, causing the prices to explode. Furniture that was considered tiresome, old, and worn out in the sixties, seventies, and eighties has been revived, and collectors are willing to pay twenty thousand dollars for a couch which only ten years ago would have been tossed in the dump by its owner.

Molesworth furniture has captured people's hearts once again, especially now that the West is in vogue. Americans feel strongly attached to their heritage. For easterners the work is cosmopolitan and chic. For westerners it is sturdy, recalling a romantic and rugged era filled with tradition.

Designed in 1951 for a good friend, this complete Molesworth interior is a paradigm of Molesworth's personal style. The room was fashioned around the owner's two original Coca-Cola calendar paintings and a third one supplied by Molesworth. The four Edward Grigware paintings on the wall feature the owner's ranch in the various seasons, and the Chevrolet emblem on the curtain is a token of the owner's profession. Copper items sharpened Molesworth's design, and he incorporated padded leather and a wainscot to give this room balance and elegance. The exacting contours of the Art Deco-style desk with its built-in radio emphasize Molesworth's affinity for high style.

Photographs © 1992 by David Swift

Photo © 1992 by David Swift

Wyoming collectors are tickled by the bright Chimayo weavings, fringe, and shiny tacks which are Molesworth trademarks. The round table, featuring the work of marquetry artist Russell Blood, is one of only three tables in this style ever sold by Molesworth. ▲

Cowboy china in this Molesworth dining room of red leather and dark fir recalls a romantic image of an elegant dude-ranch supper. The burl lamp is another playful Molesworth touch. ▶

Photo © 1992 by David Swift

REVIVAL

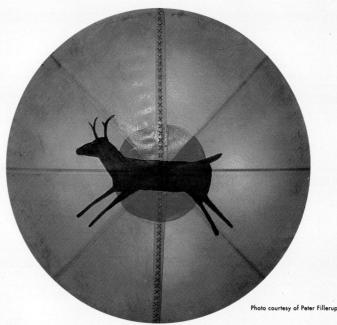

Photo courtesy of Peter Fillerup

More and more people are traveling west to vacation at dude ranches, stare wide-eyed at rodeo cowboys on bucking broncs, or challenge their city-slicker strength on cattle drives. At the most popular destination cities—Aspen, Sun Valley, Jackson Hole, and different parts of Montana—second-home buyers are finding romantic retreats from the city. Cowboy style exudes the comfort, adventure and romance that people crave.

Because of this explosion of interest in the West there has been a tremendous revival in western furniture. Suddenly, chairs covered in bright-colored Chimayo weavings, rawhide lamp shades, and pole furniture embellished with cowboy silhouettes is a lucrative style again, one that both contemporary furniture makers and interior designers across the country can capitalize on.

A new crop of furniture makers has taken the Molesworth tradition to even higher style. Driftwood table by Jimmy Covert, keyhole chairs by New West, iron tipi chandelier by Peter Fillerup.

Photo © 1992 by David Swift

53

*W*estern furniture makers and craftsmen restoring Molesworth furniture covet Molesworth tacks. While some of the tacks are readily available, the 13/16-inch hammered brass size (one that Molesworth used excessively) can no longer be purchased from supply houses, and furniture makers are hoarding the last of their cache. Molesworth used this star tack on only a handful of pieces early in his career.

*C*owboy western style can be punched up with displays of Old West antiques and collectibles, such as these vintage cowboy boots owned by Teresa and Tyler Beard of Comanche, Texas.

When Thomas Molesworth or Frank Lloyd Wright designed a home, they did it their way. Today clients work closely with furniture makers to design the pieces of furniture they would like in their home, right down to choosing the type of wood. Fir, pine, and cedar are some of the most popular choices.

Photo © 1992 by David Swift

Providing momentum behind this revival, in particular, is a colony of western furniture makers from Molesworth's home town, Cody, Wyoming. These artists are inspired by the Molesworth tradition and in their own way seek to perpetuate his romantic vision and quality craftsmanship. All in this colony are involved in restoring authentic Molesworth, making every effort to replicate his style precisely, even down to purchasing the same brand of upholstery tacks used by Molesworth forty years ago. Like modern-day Buffalo Bills, these craftsmen have tickled people's fancy about the West. They have also helped rekindle the furniture-making legacy of the cowboy.

It seems no one in the world loved and respected Tom Molesworth more than contractor and patron of the arts, Lloyd Taggart of Cody, Wyoming. As Taggart said, "old Moley" and he "hee-hawed and laughed over stories" when they were together. "Tom had a wonderful sense of humor," seventy-three year-old Taggart said. "And although he could be crabby and taciturn, he was a great artist with a lot of taste."

SWEET WATER RANCH

Inspired by Thomas Molesworth's artistic excellence, Taggart and partner Tom Roach established Sweet Water Ranch in Cody. The Sweet Water Ranch is dedicated to building quality reproductions of Molesworth's furniture. The doors of Sweet Water opened January 12, 1991, and in the first year of business, Taggart and his sons— Bryan, marketing director, and Marc in production— made great strides. Most of their clients have been second-home owners, including famous people such as Jane Fonda and Ted Turner. With six workers in the factory— including master craftsman Lester Santos—the sanding, carving, hammering, and upholstering doesn't stop.

"We're carrying on Molesworth's tradition, not interpreting it," Bryan Taggart said. "We're doing what Tom did, his designs, his things." Sweet Water's love seats, decorated with burls and lathed poles, are exactly like Molesworth originals. Most of the furniture is made of douglas fir like Molesworth's, and the wood carvings are exact down to the last shaving. Santos adds that in some ways Sweet Water Ranch furniture is better quality than Molesworth originals.

*T*he charm of the Sweet Water Ranch's furniture is the quality of its replicas. Time is spent routing out and painting some of Molesworth's exceptional relief designs, like this image of Buffalo Bill carefully imitated by craftsman Lester Santos. ◄

Thomas Molesworth used the bulging contours of a burl for design inspiration. ▼ Here Sweet Water Ranch has reproduced his style well. The table base, couch, lamp, and small table all show various effects of this unusual twist of nature. The bulbous mass of pine is then balanced in this room by more sophisticated Molesworth design ideas, such as the half-pole design around the coffee table and a gunfighter chair. The black Chimayo blanket, instead of the more common red, gives this room a cosmopolitan look. Western artwork is, of course, a natural complement to a Molesworth interior.

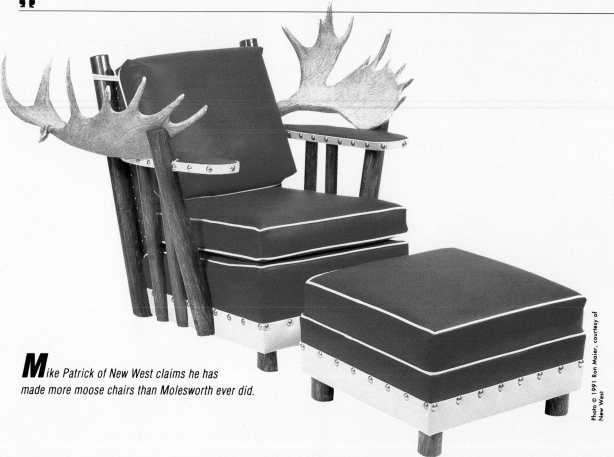

*M*ike Patrick of New West claims he has
made more moose chairs than Molesworth ever did.

MICHAEL AND VIRGINIA PATRICK OF NEW WEST

The Patricks in Cody are more interested in creating Molesworth-*inspired* pieces of furniture and accessories than exact replicas. At first glance, the Patricks' furniture and style looks just like Molesworth's, but with a little scrutiny you can't miss the spark of the Patricks' imagination. The two designers have a bottomless store of ways to make a room more fun to live in. They make the traditional Molesworth cowboy arm chair featuring a silhouette of the gunfighter, but they also designed a complementary cowgirl chair with an image of Annie Oakley. For the Boom Town Casino in Reno, Nevada, the

At first glance, many people find burls to be grotesque, but it takes a master craftsman like Thomas Molesworth to turn a burl into a balanced and attractive piece of furniture.

These bulbous aberrations are created by a virus in the trees, which causes the cells to multiply. Some tree limbs are plagued with a chain of burls, while others might have just one discreet bulge.

Amassing burls is a difficult task, especially around Cody, Wyoming, where the competition is stiff. When Molesworth was working, he sent search groups into the woods to cut down these unusual phenomena while the trees were still alive. Today, each furniture maker has a few key people—from loggers to game hunters—who gather burls for them or tip them off as to prime locations of burls. Because burls are in higher demand today, furniture makers are forced to use burls from dead limbs as well as from green ones, even though using the dead limbs is trickier because the wood has begun the decay process.

Burls are brought to the shop, where the bark is peeled to keep the bugs out. Then the green wood is left to dry for three to four years before it can be used. While the burl is seen in other styles of furniture, it is really a western trademark. Old West architects used knotty pine; one of the most famous such structures is the Million Dollar Cowboy Bar in Jackson Hole, Wyoming.

Like Molesworth, contemporary furniture makers have discovered that the fir burl, while harder to find, is stronger and more attractive than the pine burl. These wartlike creations are gathered from forests throughout the West.

New West furniture inspires unabashed visions of western fantasy. While these chairs were inspired by Molesworth's cowboy arm chair with the Edward Grigware gunfighter silhouette, the Patricks went beyond Molesworth. They created the complementary cowgirl chair in the image of Annie Oakley to make a pair.

Patricks built four bar stools with the cut-out gunfighter image on the backs with the seats and arms covered in furry cowhide. (Molesworth's chairs were never hairy.) And instead of re-producing an original Molesworth chandelier, the Patricks designed their own version: Rodeo Days. The chandelier, sixteen feet high with a twenty-four-inch diameter, is adorned with steel figures such as a cowboy roping a cow, another cowboy sitting on an arena fence, and a clown holding an umbrella. New West has even gone so far as to put tiny copper spurs on the heels of the cowboys.

New West's rodeo chandelier embraces the whimsical and irreverent West.

Photo courtesy of New West

__N__ew West's painted cabinet is made of lodgepole pine, adorned with antler and burl, and was painted by equine artist Lana Peratti. This charming piece, which brings the outdoors inside, could work well in any room.

Photo © 1992 by David Swift

KEN SIGGINS OF TRIANGLE Z RANCH FURNITURE

As Sweet Water Ranch and New West continue to produce loads of furniture to satiate the designers' appetite for the Old West, one Cody man is impervious to the hustle and bustle of the rage—but no less important. Hidden in his shop at the base of the Absaroka Mountains at the end of a bumpy dirt road, Ken Siggins is turning out quality lodgepole pieces for a loyal clientele that he has cultivated for thirty years.

Triangle Z Ranch Furniture has become part of the landscape in Cody. Many dude ranches up and down the North and South Fork are furnished with Siggins's work and forty of his lodgepole-and-rawhide chairs smarten the Proud Cut Saloon, one of the most popular places to dine in Cody. He has also built tables and chairs for Tom Brokaw's second home in Montana, created furniture for a posh New York office and conference room on Wall Street, and sent furniture to a ski lodge in Maine and a home in Hawaii.

Ken Siggins has been most important in the western furniture tradition because when business was lean in the sixties and no one else in Cody was making furniture, he handled the demand for furniture and repairs on Molesworth pieces. Probably more Molesworth has passed through Siggins's hands than any others.

Cowboy decor isn't only for a person's second home in the West. Russ Fraser commissioned Ken Siggins to build furniture for his New York office at Fitch Investor's Service. The rugged environment, featuring Siggins tooled-leather club chairs, is an easy reminder to Fraser of his many trips out West. ▼

Siggins' ranch furniture turns Russ Fraser's meeting room into a comfortable work environment. ◄

It wasn't always easy riding the economic roller-coaster, he admits, but when business was lean he relied on real-estate pursuits. He stayed with furniture building because there was always a need for furniture in the area and he grew to enjoy the craft.

Siggins's personal contribution to the cowboy style can't be ignored. While he studied the basic shapes of Molesworth furniture, he preferred to keep his work more useful than stylish, or "cowboy deco." His wood pieces are generally without decoration, but he was also the first furniture maker in Cody to apply tooled leather to side panels of the club chair design. His own living room, a showroom for his work, is furnished in solid fir furniture. Each piece is simple in design and looks as if it might outlast his grandchildren's grandchildren. While Siggins enjoys using burls, the bulk of his furniture is made of lodgepole, cut in such a way as to reflect sensuous natural curves. Many of his tables maintain rough edges that show off the natural texture of the wood. His rustic living room is highlighted with a rawhide lamp shade on a base made of a bighorn sheep horn and a contorted piece of driftwood.

The chair with woven hide back and seat is a common style in western decor. The simplicity and strength of this piece makes the work a sturdy option for a ranch kitchen or dining room.

Jimmy and Lynda Covert
stand in their shop behind one
of Jimmy's finest driftwood
pieces. Fir and juniper-cedar
driftwood is his favorite
medium. "A piece of driftwood
has something magic in it, a
life of its own," Covert said. In
the back of his mind his goal
is always to make each piece
of furniture friendly, a piece
which makes you feel good
when you look at it. He was so
successful with this bench that
it begs for stroking. The
sensual lines could work
elegantly inside a home, or the
bench could be an exclusive
retreat for watching sunsets.

JIMMY COVERT

In 1980 Siggins hired apprentice Jimmy Covert. Camped out in a lean-to in the South Fork Valley, Covert rode his mule Willie to the Triangle Z Ranch Furniture shop every day. Sometimes Covert would just sit among the trees and look over the valley, enjoying a morning sunrise or an evening sunset. He claims the solitude inspired his work. In his spare time Covert experimented with more free-form works out of driftwood, which would later become his signature.

Now owner of his own shop in Cody, Jimmy Covert makes furniture with impeccable craftsmanship. His ir-

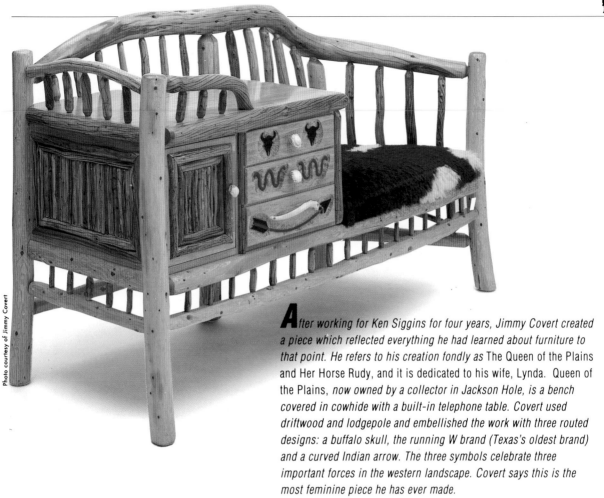

*A*fter working for Ken Siggins for four years, Jimmy Covert created a piece which reflected everything he had learned about furniture to that point. He refers to his creation fondly as The Queen of the Plains and Her Horse Rudy, and it is dedicated to his wife, Lynda. Queen of the Plains, *now owned by a collector in Jackson Hole, is a bench covered in cowhide with a built-in telephone table. Covert used driftwood and lodgepole and embellished the work with three routed designs: a buffalo skull, the running W brand (Texas's oldest brand) and a curved Indian arrow. The three symbols celebrate three important forces in the western landscape. Covert says this is the most feminine piece he has ever made.*

regular driftwood pieces inspire lofty musings about nature, the environment, and the meaning of the true West. His designs challenge the straight lines of contemporary furniture and embrace the sensuous curves of driftwood indigenous to the Cody area. When a piece is finished, the work is a celebration of organic form and the undulation of light and dark variations in the wood.

Outside Cody, Wyoming, there are a myriad of furniture makers creating works which have been inspired by Molesworth or simply by their love of the West and its current popularity. Craftspeople are proliferating in other parts of Wyoming, Montana, Oregon, California, New Mexico, Arizona and Texas.

Photos © 1992 Scott McKinley

Roy Fisk

Some artisans, such as Roy Fisk of Bondurant, Wyoming, only turn out a few quality pieces a year. Fisk is interested in the craft of making furniture. He meticulously pieces poles together in a mosaic, much as the early craftsmen of the Adirondacks did. He wants his furniture to look rugged and classy and is averse to turning out anything really commercial.

This Adirondack-style liquor cabinet, ▶ hand-crafted by Wyoming craftsman Roy Fisk, is the second piece he ever made and a wonderful example of folk art. Fisk is meticulous about keeping his work intricate yet rugged. He hand selects lodgepole pine for its attractive worm tracks and likes to carve wildlife insets, like the one above. Fisk's furniture is available through Fighting Bear Antiques.

JOHN MORTENSEN OF MORTENSEN STUDIOS

An innovative new western furniture design has come from John Mortensen in Salt Lake City. A renowned western sculptor, he has created cut-out sculptured reliefs cast in bronze. The sculptured panels are then used as table stands, chair backs or lamp stands in his Rainbow Trail Collection. The tabletops are made of sandstone, glass, or sometimes wood. Mortensen also designs wood reliefs which are carved by Bart Walker of Driggs, Idaho.

Western sculptor John Mortensen has recently turned his hand to furniture design. His silhouette reliefs incorporated into lamps, tables, and chairs, are an innovative way to display western art in an interior.

Photo © 1992 by David Swift, courtesy of Martin Harris Gallery

Photo courtesy of Willow Run Woodworking

A *Charles Ringer moving sculpture decorates Rob Mazza's Molesworth-inspired sideboard.*

The side table to the right by Rob Mazza was purchased by actor Jeff Bridges for his Montana home.

ROB MAZZA OF WILLOW RUN WOODWORKING

From his shop in Belgrade, Montana, Rob Mazza features cowboy and wildlife images on his lodgepole-pine pieces. Sometimes he uses a routed silhouette and other times will cut out the design. The iron drawer pulls on this sideboard illustrate this craftsman's attention to detail and high style.

Photo © 1992 by Rick Harrison, courtesy of Rustic Furniture

DIANE COLE OF RUSTIC FURNITURE

In Bozeman, Montana, Diane Cole crafts Adirondack willow and western pole pieces. She adapts the Adirondack style by incorporating wood slats and featuring Montana picture rock as centerpieces in willow-mosaic tabletops. She is particularly interested in showing off Mother Nature's sensuous curves.

74

Photo courtesy of L. D. Burke

L. D. BURKE

The cowboy style is also proliferating in the Southwest. Mavericks such as L. D. Burke of Santa Fe, New Mexico, are leading the trend. In many respects these furniture builders and a new crop of designers are turning to the cowboy look as a way to complement or substitute the Santa Fe style.

Every one of Burke's creations is a celebration of art and craftsmanship learned over a thirty-year period. He builds one-of-a-kind tables, chairs, bureaus, beds, wall hanging/collages, children's furniture, and signature mirrors decorated with western memorabilia and words of cowboy wisdom. He has received over 175 national and international awards for interiors and graphic design and is collected by stars such as rocker Jimmy Messina and other well-to-do.

In 1990 L. D. Burke started designing a line of children's furniture. One of his clients spent $17,000 on Burke's children's furniture. The room included a queen bed, two end tables, two lamps, a tall dresser embellished with cow horns, a ten-foot long cabinet, a chair, a six-foot long hat, gun and tack rack, and a horn floor hat rack. These pieces have a tactile quality that little kids and cowboys can't keep their hands off of, Burke says. ▲

Intrigued with Burke's imagination, musician Jimmy Messina (of Loggins and Messina) purchased this gun lamp and continues to collect Burke's work. ▶

L.D. Burke's whimsical art pieces give a room western pizzazz. ▼

RON MCGEE OF WILD WEST FURNITURE AND SUPPLY

*R*on McGee's beds are built to withstand a 250-pound football player and sometimes even a car, he says. With free artistic license, McGee built these pieces for Tex Earnhardt's bunkhouse in southeastern Arizona: two bunks, a chest of drawers with barbed-wire drawer pulls, a couple of lodgepole hat racks with horse-bit and horn hooks, and a set of curtain rods with steer-head silhouettes on the end.

Dressed in a black cowboy hat, a button-down shirt, Wranglers and boots, Ron McGee of Apache Junction, Arizona, is another maverick with a unique approach to furniture making. He looks like he should be herding cattle on the range, not peddling his furniture at posh designer stores around the country. McGee has been building western furniture for only a few years, and collecting western memorabilia for more than ten. His work is available in galleries, designer shops around the West and at his home. It reflects his wacky imagination and familiarity with the cowboy life. For his home in Sun Valley, Hollywood star Bruce Willis purchased a McGee bed crafted from an old western wagon.

McGee says the white walls, pastel furniture, and glass tables of the popular Southwest style make him uncomfortable. "I make the kind of furniture a cowboy can put his feet on and spit on," he said.

A family room at the Lazy EX Ranch in Chandler, Arizona, owned by Tex and Pam Earnhardt, features furniture and accessories by Ron McGee. The sand tables recall the ceremonial practice and art of the Navajo, Hopi and Pueblo Indians of creating symbolic designs with varicolored sand on a flat surface. McGee also designed the rusted-steel gunfighter lamp that sits on the end table.

Most of Ron McGee's furniture is made of what he calls manufactured barnwood. After collecting most of his own wood, primarily Ponderosa pine, McGee peels the bark, sands the wood and constructs a chair, table, or bed frame. Each piece is built to last. Then he paints the piece of furniture with his "funky finish," a mixture of green, red, and brown. With more sandpaper, he rubs the painted wood to give it a rugged chipped-paint look. To complement the old look, he uses rusty branding irons for braces instead of new steel. And if he uses a silver conch for decoration, he makes sure the conch is dull, not polished. Quality and sturdiness are McGee's bywords, but don't confuse that with perfection: a scratch or nick in the wood can improve the charm of a piece.

Photo © 1992 by Elyse Lewin, as appeared in *Home Magazine*

*J*erry England's kitchen features his own gunfighter chairs, matched with his cowboy sweetheart chairs. The border of brands gives this room a home-on-the-range warmth.

JERRY ENGLAND OF LURE OF THE DIM TRAILS

With a similar cowboy spirit, Jerry England of Woodland Hills, California, is building furniture and accessories. His business is named for a beloved 1907 book by B. M. Bower. While England's work is influenced by the Molesworth style, he has added more decoration, and his interior designs are often embellished with authentic cowboy memorabilia hanging from the walls and displayed on shelves. He has also designed fabric for couches with images of buffalo, cowboy hats, cacti and tipis.

Photo © 1992 by Elyse Lewin, as appeared in *Home Magazine*

When Jerry England's son announced he was getting married, England thought it would be fun to build his daughter-in-law a hope chest, keeping alive a family tradition begun by England's grandfather. That was his first piece, and since then, England's head has been kicking and spinning with new cowboy images and furniture designs.

Milo Marks fills each longhorn with resin and corks it to give the hollow horn stability. He then matches the horns in sets as closely as he can to give his work physical and artistic balance. Once the horn has been sanded, finished and bolted to a frame and tabletop, Marks's furniture bears a distinctly western look, reminiscent of the 1880s, when longhorn furniture was popular in Texas (and even before that in Europe). ▶

For Jerry England the silhouette is an important element in a cowboy interior. The images of cowboys and Indians on the range bring the drama of Hollywood westerns into this bedroom. ◀

MILO AND TEDDI MARKS OF WESTERN HERITAGE DESIGNS

In Meridian, Texas, Milo and Teddi Marks are making contemporary horn furniture, inspired by early longhorn craftsmen. The pair also create natural wood pieces with carvings such as a steer head. "Our stuff is so sturdy you can do the Texas Two-Step on it," Teddi Marks said.

The Markses have been in the antique business since 1968 and only in the last five years have been working on perfecting their longhorn designs. Their largest sales are made when traveling the rodeo circuit. Clint Johnson, three-time World Champion Bronc Rider is one of their fans and collects their work.

A longghorn table crafted by Milo Marks is both
a rustic and elegant addition to an interior.

*T*his steer-head bench made by Western
Heritage Designs illustrates rustic elegance
with a hint of whimsy.

Photo © 1992 by David Swift

Lynda Covert, has her own leather and upholstery shop in Cody, Wyoming. She uses her husband's hand-peeled bench as a showcase for her pillows of leather and untamed fringe. Lynda has designed a series of pillows with a trapunto and applique gunfighter.

ACCESSORIES

Accessories are a key to the cowboy style. Often these decorative pieces bear the western icons such as silhouettes of cowboys, tipis, and wildlife. Other accessories show off textured fabrics or incorporate western memorabilia—boots, horseshoes, barbed wire and the like. These artifacts can be turned into lamp bases, wall hangings, hat and coat racks, or simply used as decorative items on a shelf or end table.

As the western style develops, accessory-makers are popping up everywhere. Fireplace screens, andirons, antler chandeliers, cowboy-boot lamps, barn-wood frames, and ornamented mirrors are some of the more popular decoratives. Other accessories include pillows, quilts, and fabric designs.

Photo courtesy of Jimmy Covert

Metal artisan Peter Fillerup of Heber, Utah, collaborated with Jimmy Covert on this two-sided desk to create the sculptured relief.

Interior designers are also helping perpetuate the western dream. Often the designer is a liaison between the furniture maker and the client. Particularly in Los Angeles, design shops have helped perpetuate the style among movie stars such as Whoopie Goldberg, Jeff Bridges, and Patrick Swayze, who are using the style in their homes and second homes or ranches. Other celebrities interested in the western style, in particular designer Linda Niven's collection at the Ranch in Aspen, include Goldie Hawn, Jill St. John, Arnold Schwarzenegger, John Oats, and Barbara Walters.

Designers are more than a marketing link; they develop innovative ways to incorporate the furniture and style into interiors. Sometimes a designer will rely mainly on a furniture maker's style and embellish the room with iron accessories and Navajo rugs to create a room much like Molesworth would have done. Other times a

A chicken incubator in your living room? Designer Hilary Heminway of Connecticut and Montana asks, "Why not?" For a sophisticated Montana home, she turned a chicken incubator into a coffee table and placed it between two lodgepole-pine couches built by Cody furniture maker Ken Siggins. In this western room she used an old wooden sled as a table to complement one of Siggins's lodgepole day beds, painted in a pickle green. Both the incubator and the sled are humorous pieces whose textures give these western interiors warmth and depth, Heminway feels. They also are convincing evidence that buying just the so-called "in" western furniture is not the only way to create a comfortable and whimsical environment. ▶

*D*esigner Judy Singleton, of Mountain House Designs in Jackson Hole, Wyoming, worked with her client to achieve a western atmosphere. Here the designer has mixed an L. D. Burke armoire with a Jimmy Covert rocker and two-sided desk, a moose-antler coffee table by Elkhorn Design, and a leather couch. ▲

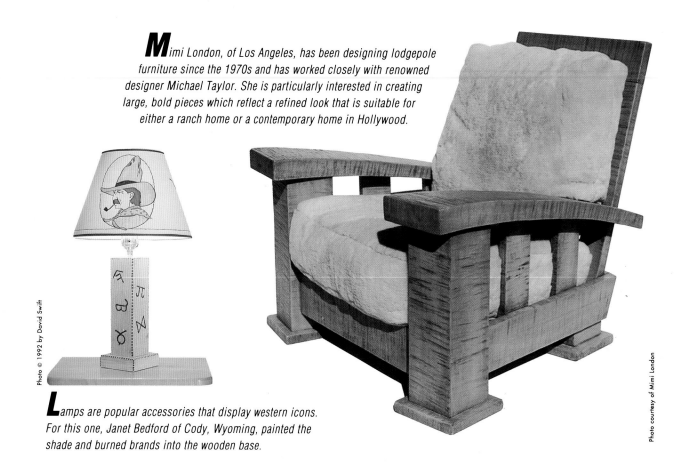

Mimi London, of Los Angeles, has been designing lodgepole furniture since the 1970s and has worked closely with renowned designer Michael Taylor. She is particularly interested in creating large, bold pieces which reflect a refined look that is suitable for either a ranch home or a contemporary home in Hollywood.

Photo © 1992 by David Swift

Photo courtesy of Mimi London

Lamps are popular accessories that display western icons. For this one, Janet Bedford of Cody, Wyoming, painted the shade and burned brands into the wooden base.

designer will use only a token piece of furniture along with a few cowboy accessories to create a room with a western aura. Finally, the challenge for designers is mixing styles to create an eclectic western, but original look which blends with various architecture and interior dimensions.

The western style inspires whimsy and imagination, combines elements of the landscape, and encourages recycling. Designer Hilary Heminway of Connecticut and Montana turned a chicken incubator into a coffee table and used a Flexible Flyer sled as a coffee table in a Montana ranch house. Linda Bedell of Aspen, Colorado, found remnants of cowboy linoleum for the floor of her child's room, and Astrid Sommer of San Francisco mounted deer horns on two red blocks of wood to hold a curtain rod. In this era of high-tech and harried lifestyles, the western style appeals for its romantic image of slower-paced living and simplicity. An interior furnished with cowboy whimsy, sensuousness, and fine craftsmanship lets us revive the romantic western dream.

Designer Linda Bedell of Aspen, Colorado, embraces a western eclectic style. In this room featuring nineteen pairs of antique skis, she mixes cowhide sofas with leather lacing, a Jimmy Covert coffee table, and a Mimi London chair. The back wall features a Tramp Art chest, original Edward Curtis photographs, and Peter Fillerup lanterns.

Photo © 1992 by Dave Marlow, courtesy of Linda Bedell

*L*eather and lodgepole combine the best of cowboy and rustic in the Tyler and Teresa Beard living room. The lodgepole sofa frames were made by Lodgepole Furniture in Jackson Hole, Wyoming. The leather cushions and pillows were custom orders from a boot maker. The base of the floor lamp is also from Lodgepole Furniture, and the stretched rawhide lamp shade was created by Taos Drum in Santa Fe, New Mexico. The small rustic tables by the sofa sides are by Sam Bair.

GALLERY
OF WESTERN FURNITURE
AND ACCESSORIES

Inspired by the rugged and romantic life of the cowboy hero, interior designers have turned the very basic elements of his lifestyle into cowboy couture. What a working cowboy considers necessary tools, such as a rope, branding iron, or set of spurs, designers consider as treasured pieces of nostalgia, for their marvelous texture and captivating design potential.

Cowboy furniture is made of wood native to the West. It employs bold and rich colors, western silhouette images and Indian crafts and natural textures. The style embraces simplicity and comfort, sparkles with whimsy, and is usually animated in some way by cowboy and Indian heroics. Above all the style emerges from the landscape and the history of the Old West. Often furniture or interior walls and architecture are treated to look old and rustic—and like a barrel chair, cowboy boot bookends and branding-iron candlesticks, many of the accessory objects come from the surroundings and what might be lying out in the barn.

By using these old items, native materials, textured fabrics, a combination of subtle and dramatic hues, and well-crafted wood furniture, a designer creates an ambiance which celebrates both nature and western culture.

Pop artist Bill Schenck bought a 1939 cabin built by the Wort brothers, moved it to his own property in Jackson Hole, and named it the Rubber Snake Ranch. In keeping with the rough-hewn architecture Schenck created the quintessential western lodge interior with indigenous furniture, early western paintings, and American Indian artifacts. He also decorated with beaded Indian jewelry and Navajo textiles, pre-1930. At the back of the room, Schenck built a bookcase out of contorted lodgepole. The cowhide couch is an old day bed from Struthers Burt's Bar BC Ranch in Jackson. Schenck designed a back for the piece, covered it in cowhide, and designed a complementary coffee table, built by Butch Crist of Jackson Hole.

Photo © 1992 by David Swift

A contemporary couch upholstered with two army blankets costing $10 is complemented by two Molesworth chairs and two Molesworth lamps in a remodeled Wyoming ranch home. The blanket decorating the couch is an antique lap robe used to keep sleigh riders' legs warm.   The interior design for this home is by Robert K. Lewis of New York. ▲

▶ In her family's Montana Ranch living room designer Hilary Heminway demonstrates how she models western interiors on the landscape. She likes the viewer's eye to rove up and down like it does in nature. Pictures don't have to be hung at the same height, and furniture is interesting to look at when it occupies a variety of heights in a room. Heminway uses natural hues which blend with views of mountains, hayfields, and a river seen through the window.

A fan of Hopalong Cassidy and Larry McMurtry, Californian Jerry England loves to surround himself with cowboy memorabilia. He owns more than 200 western videos and has an extraordinary collection of western artifacts to complement his own hand-crafted Cowboy Chic furniture. The couches featured in this den sport England's original fabric called Home on the Range. The fabric is inspired by silhouettes of tipis, buffalo and cowboy hats. The silhouettes on the table were carved, then painted. While many of the silhouettes used on his furniture were inspired by Molesworth designs, England also studies the art of Charlie Russell and Edward Borein for design ideas.

*A*n aspen-bark lamp designed by Jackson Hole craftsman Rick Horn, casts a warm glow in Bill Schenck's dark, masculine cabin. While others have tried to replicate this lamp with thinly cut pine, the look isn't nearly as delicate and unusual. ▶

Interior Designer Andrea Lawrence Wood creates a western look by using indigenous wood, western tack, a horn chair, and a variety of textured fabrics such as this leather couch and her textile pillows.▼

*B*edazzled with New West's custom work, owners of the Star Hill Ranch in Wapiti, Wyoming, had the furniture company design and furnish their interiors. The lodge and six cabins are decorated with New West beds, bureaus, chairs, lamps, chandeliers, and fire screens. And each cabin—instead of being labeled boys' cabin, girls' cabin—bears the Lakota Indian name for an animal indigenous to the area. Outside the cabin doors, New West installed steel lamps featuring the creature and followed through inside with the theme on the beds and light fixtures. The owners of this ranch found the Patricks of New West a delight to work with. They were full of ideas, produced quality furniture, and had the lodge and six cabins completely decorated in four months.

*R*ay Thurston, elected 1992 Arizona Entrepreneur of the Year, furnished his get-away cabin in Jackson Hole, Wyoming, with Molesworth furniture and 1940 lodgepole furniture crafted by local craftsman Bob Kranenberg. To give his cabin romance and a rustic ambiance, he included a forty-four-inch wrought-iron chandelier and sconces, custom designed by Fighting Bear Enterprises of Jackson. He has also decorated his cabin with Navajo rugs, Pendleton blankets, and cowboy and Indian artifacts. All the Molesworth furniture was found and re-upholstered by Fighting Bear Antiques in Jackson Hole. ◀ Photo © 1992 by David Swift

▲ This Molesworth-inspired chandelier, designed by Fighting Bear Enterprises, was cut with a scroll saw and the individual pieces have a hammered profile instead of two-dimensional surface like most of the metalwork being done today. The tipi and shield are painted rawhide. Metal fabrication is executed by craftsman Tom Reifschneider of Jackson Hole.

North American wildlife motifs are important in western interiors. This iron sconce, made by Bill Feeley of Cody, is an exquisite piece of art as well as a functional lamp. ◄

Diane Cole's willow furniture, crafted to reflect nature's innate spirituality, blends well with an antique Adirondack chair inside this rustic cabin. Cole's lamp with a willow base and rawhide shade illuminates the room. ►

This fireplace screen is a Molesworth-inspired creation by Fighting Bear Antiques of Jackson Hole, Wyoming.▼

Photo © 1991 by Chris Cassatt

With little financial restraint, Molesworth was able to create one of the most exquisite western escapes. The furniture in this lodge, now owned by Laura Hunt, is the finest collection of Molesworth in private hands. ▲

▶ This glassed-in porch features a 19th-century buffalo head peering over American Reed Furniture from the 1920s-30s and a hickory chair with original paint. The room also holds an old peeling cowboy chair and a cowhide. Designed by Robert K. Lewis.

Photo © 1992 by David Swift

Photo © 1992 by David Swift

Photo © 1992 by David Swift

*J*immy and Lynda Covert work as a husband-and-wife team to advance and interpret western style. While they have been influenced by Molesworth's design, they boldly pursue their own creativity. This red club chair; alias the Tipi Chair, built by Jimmy Covert and upholstered by Lynda Covert, is an example of one of their finest collaborations. Lynda's simple geometric tipi design decorating red leather cushion complements the rustic curves of Jimmy's chair. The entire effect is simple yet fanciful, rustic yet cosmopolitan. The driftwood chair, lamp and table demonstrate Jimmy's keen artistic sensibility that takes him beyond Molesworth's style. A funky old Victorian lamp and the red Navajo rug also add a passionate twist to the traditional western fashion. ▲

◄ A Valley Ranch cabin furnished in Triangle Z Ranch Furniture. The wall has been treated to look rustic.

► A fireplace is often the center of a sitting room. This one, made of moss stone collected in the Jackson Hole area, also provides winter recreation for the owner and builder, Bruce Simon, who has attached a carabiner to the top and uses his hand-made fireplace as a climbing wall. Moving around the buck's antlers is tricky, he says.
Photo ©1992 by David Swift

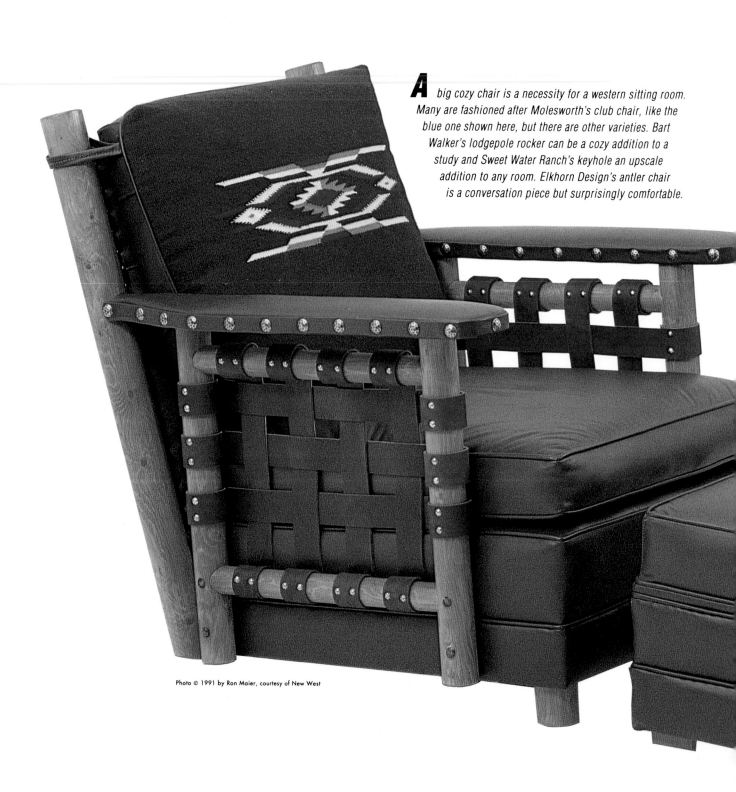

A big cozy chair is a necessity for a western sitting room. Many are fashioned after Molesworth's club chair, like the blue one shown here, but there are other varieties. Bart Walker's lodgepole rocker can be a cozy addition to a study and Sweet Water Ranch's keyhole an upscale addition to any room. Elkhorn Design's antler chair is a conversation piece but surprisingly comfortable.

Photo © 1991 by Ron Maier, courtesy of New West

Photo courtesy of Sweet Water Ranch

Photo courtesy of Elkhorn Design

Photo courtesy of Bart Walker

Jimmy Covert chose to incorporate bronze-relief images by Peter Fillerup into his version of a western-style writing desk.

Inspired by Molesworth's two-sided desk design, Mike Patrick of New West created a one-sided writing desk with a complementary key-hole chair. Instead of routing a cowboy design on the piece, Patrick used leather, tacks, and paint to create the effect.◄

Molesworth's club chairs and large leather couches are a comfy invitation to relax and enjoy a quiet afternoon. ▼

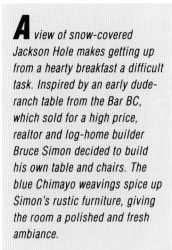

A view of snow-covered Jackson Hole makes getting up from a hearty breakfast a difficult task. Inspired by an early dude-ranch table from the Bar BC, which sold for a high price, realtor and log-home builder Bruce Simon decided to build his own table and chairs. The blue Chimayo weavings spice up Simon's rustic furniture, giving the room a polished and fresh ambiance.

Simon, who built his own cabin, has applied a crisscross pattern on the cabinets. The pattern repeats throughout the interior on doors and on counter chairs. Photo © 1992 by David Swift ▶

▼ Morning sunlight dances in Jimmy and Lynda Covert's dining room, a corner of simple elegance in Cody, Wyoming. The four gunfighter chairs are Molesworth reproductions by Jimmy Covert and the sideboard against the wall is Covert's original design. The sideboard is adorned with bronze pulls by Peter Fillerup.

Photo © 1992 by David Swift

*B*url bar-back, made by Jackson woodworker Jack Kranenberg for the Million Dollar Cowboy Bar, now holds Bill Schenck's original Wallace Rodeo Pattern china. In the 1940s and '50s, most dude ranches and diners in the West served their hot grub on plates decorated with bucking broncs, swinging ropes, cattle, saddles, cowboy hats and a hodgepodge of brands and other cowboy symbols. Western china was not so much "in" as a necessity of the business. Now collectors are sleuthing through antique stores for the remains of these valuable china services. A five-piece, eight-place setting of Wallace western china with serving pieces, all signed by artist Til Goodan and bearing the stamp Westward Ho, can cost anywhere from $4,000 to $7,500.

Photo © 1992 by David Swift

COMPATIBLE WOODS

A western interior usually features wood which is native to the area. Lodgepole furniture, crafted from pine or fir, is the most common ingredient of a western room. Furniture makers also use native willow, cedar, or old barn wood. Other woods that blend comfortably are oak, walnut and hickory. Many kinds of antique wood pieces, whether painted or weathered, also fit nicely into a cowboy interior.

A Victorian oak table standing on a braided rug is the centerpiece of this rustic western dining room. Designer Astrid Sommer has created the western interior with two Old Hickory chairs, a German Town rug, Indian prints, papoose baskets, two decorative canoes, and a shelf of North American Indian baskets and cowboy china. The bear sculpture standing on a rustic stand in the corner of the room is a reproduction of the classic bears from Bern, Switzerland, which were sold in Yellowstone at the turn of the century.

Photo courtesy of Tyler and Teresa Beard and True West

Responding to the demand for collectible western china—used from the 1940s to the early '60s in dude ranches and coffee shops across the frontier—Tyler and Teresa Beard have purchased the Wallace China trademark, Westward Ho, and are now producing exact reproductions of the old china. A place setting by the Beards costs about one-third as much as buying an antique set of original Wallace. The only difference is that the reproduction china does not bear Till Goodan's signature.

*T*yler and Teresa Beard creatively combine new and old pieces for a comfortable cowboy bedroom. The sturdy bed frame is made of peeled pole. (The work of this particular furniture maker is available only through Antēks in Dallas and Homestead in Fredericksburg, TX.) The western look is enhanced by the addition of Navajo blankets on the bed and a rustic night table by furniture maker Sam Bair. The stretched rawhide lamp shade was created by Taos Drum and the lamp base is made from an old copper rodeo trophy of the type that small-town rodeos handed out. ◀

Inspired by his admiration for a rustic bed built by his grandfather, Ken Siggins started building ranch furniture. His son Austin loves this bed and small chair his father made for him. ▶

Photo © 1992 by David Swift

Designer Astrid Sommer discovered that the footboard panels of this pine bed were "natural panels for Molesworth silhouettes." She engaged San Francisco artist Carol Anne Haggerty to paint faux inlays of Molesworth designs. The bed is covered with a Third Phase Chief's blanket. Indian artifacts—an Apache tray, a water jug, a Navajo blanket on the wall and Navajo rugs on the floor—create a romantic western ambiance. ◄

A simple bed set in this streamlined room of a ranch home is stark, like a cowboy bunk room, yet the room boasts modern architectural contours and dimensions. ▲

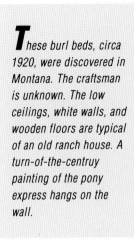

These burl beds, circa 1920, were discovered in Montana. The craftsman is unknown. The low ceilings, white walls, and wooden floors are typical of an old ranch house. A turn-of-the-centruy painting of the pony express hangs on the wall.

*B*ayley Sullivan of Woodside, California, sporting her namesake Bayley Bonnet, smiles with glee from her lodgepole crib, a custom design by Astrid Sommer and built by Bart Walker of Driggs, Idaho. ◄

▼ Astrid Sommer enhanced the western look of a Molesworth bed and chair by the addition of an 1865 tool box decorated with folk art starbursts (courtesy Showcase Antiques, Jackson Hole) and a cowhide rug. The cowboy-and-Indian scenic and moose paintings on the walls bring the outdoors inside, and pillows fashioned from feed sacks make this a fun room for kids.

*L*ily and Wolf Schlien of Textile Communications spice up their quilt designs with vibrant color and western action. In particular they are inspired by the subtle hues of the desert and the dramatic colors of the foothills of the Sangre de Cristo Mountains, near their home in Santa Fe. In this quilt, "One Always Gets Away," a cowboy twirling a rope over his head charges across the desert in pursuit of a temperamental steer. Along with the scenes based on posterized western images from the 1930s, the Schliens use Indian fetish figures, Mimbres and Indian geometric designs.

Photo courtesy Textile Communications

*T*his bedroom, designed by Hilary Heminway for a Montana fishing camp, features a Jimmy Covert bed made of logs and barn wood. A wooden hat on the wall adds a touch of whimsy.
Photo © 1992 Billy Cunningham

TEXTURE

One of the most attractive qualities about a western room is its tactile personality. Furniture makers are always talking about the sensuality of the wood they work with and designers about bringing the texture of nature indoors. Using wood which is hand-peeled and shows worm-hole patterns keeps a room rustic and interesting. Navajo blankets, cowhide rugs, leather couches, Indian baskets, iron accessories, horns, and woven rugs are appealing to the touch. Old bridles, bits, western saddles, fringed chaps and spurs also exude rugged western ambiance. Walls are another place for innovation: grass-cloth, adobe and textured wood are just a few plausible options.

*T*ooled leather and pine make a striking combination. The antlers and turquoise stone add a touch of whimsy that is part of the cowboy furniture tradition.▶
▼ "Ironsides," with head and footboards of pine, is framed in rusted iron and topped by brass balls. The elk motif in the headboard softens the overall look. Both beds designed by Mary Whitesides.

Photos courtesy Mary Whitesides

Photo courtesy New West

*H*eadboard and footboard by the Patricks of New West brings the outdoors feeling inside with rich green leather and forest scenics carved in relief.

*T*his Jerry England bedroom suite boasts his mythic silhouetttes which take us back to the times when the cowboy was the great American hero. ▲

▶ The routed designs and palisading of the half-poles gives this Molesworth bed a rustic and elegant facade.

▼ Molesworth vanity featuring a variety of cut-out handles is part of a three-piece set including a bed and dresser. The cut-out wooden shade lights the room with romantic silhouettes.

Photo courtesy of True West

Handcrafted of etched steel and art glass, these buckaroo wall sconces cast a soft glow reminiscent of a campfire.

COWBOY AND INDIAN SILHOUETTES

If you can't afford a Russell or Remington sculpture or painting, using the silhouette is an easy way to corral western images indoors. Whether routed on a piece of furniture, emblazoned on fabric, or cut out of metal, the silhouette image of the cowboy gives a room an aura of whimsy, romance and irreverence that the West is known for. The silhouette also is a tool designers use to develop theme rooms such as the cowboy room or the buffalo room, which are popular elements of western design.

*L*ace pillows, branding iron candle sticks, a 1930 Pendleton blanket, and a Sioux war shirt circa 1890 are delicate complements to Ray Thurston's Molesworth bed featuring carved panels. Photo © 1992 by David Swift

133

Photo © 1992 by David Swift

Photo © 1992 by David Swift, courtesy of The Great Bear Ranch

*D*esigner Cynthis Hackett of Qué Pasa and Yippie-ei-o created a western powder room with Yippie-ei-o fabric (available through interior designers) and lassoed the effect with rope. A set of barn-wood mirrors and a cabinet were crafted by Ron McGee to accessorize the room. ◄

Photo © 1991 by Mark Boisclair, courtesy Southwest Sampler magazine

▲ Designer Robin Weiss of Jackson Hole, Wyoming created a western powder room. She placed a sink in an old barrel painted green, and framed the mirror with a yoke. The western fixtures balance well with the unusual petroglyph wall-paper.

▼ Here an old horse bit made a perfect toilet paper holder. The iron horse hook was designed by Fighting Bear Enterprises.

► By hanging old iron pieces on the wall in a collage, designer Marty Frenkel succeeded in giving this room a textured appeal. An L. D. Burke sink and mirror, emblazoned with rope, spurs, and the saying "Thank You For Coming," add further tactile accents.

Photo courtesy of Rituals

*B*y mixing Gustav Stickley chairs with Molesworth pieces, a private collector has captured an exciting era in American furniture design. In fact, Molesworth was inspired by many other furniture makers of the Craftsman era, especially in furniture dimensions and in the use of elements such as tacks and shiny leather.

MIXING STYLES

For some tastes, a room furnished entirely in western furniture and accessories can be overwhelming. When putting together the elements of a western room, no one wants to feel she can't include her favorite Chinese antique or Victorian chair. With a little imagination, however, a living room can look western without a set of Molesworth couches, chairs, lamps, tables and ashtrays. If you like a piece well enough, there is always a place for it in your home.

It is typical to find Victorian pieces in a western setting. At the turn of the century, many posh hotels in the West, such as the Jerome in Aspen, Colorado, were furnished in Victorian to attract wealthy sportsmen and tourists who were tired of the dust and grit they encountered when traveling by train and wagon.

Other furniture styles that are commonly mixed with western are Arts and Crafts, Country, Adirondack, Monterey, Old Hickory, and Southwest. Tramp Art—small chests, stools, lamps, and boxes made of Popsicle sticks, marbles, chipped wood, and glass—is also a compatible addition to a western interior. All styles share the similar charm of rustic America. Together the pieces can provide an eclectic ambiance rich in natural wood and rugged shapes.

A bronze sculpture by John Mortensen is the center of this western living room, designed by Mortensen and his wife Pam. John has recently created a line of furniture that incorporates bronze castings of images inspired by three western symbols: the cowboy, wildlife and petroglyphs. Mortensen's work is hand-forged and crafted in the tradition of the great ranches and lodges of the West. The sturdy furniture complements the antler couch from an old Jackson Hole dude ranch, circa 1920, and a romantic Victorian couch.

"**W**hen designing a western interior it is desirable to mix the old and the new, the traditional and avant garde," says designer Marty Frenkel of Rituals. Here a Mission desk is adorned with a Tramp Art box, mirror and frame. The table also holds an Arts and Crafts lamp, a nineteenth-century Peruvian vase, and a nineteenth-century iron. ▶

◀ A reproduction of a Molesworth chandelier by Buffalo Studios hangs over an original Gustav Stickley dining table and a set of antique English Arts and Crafts chairs in designer Linda Bedell's home.

Tramp Art has recently been rediscovered by many collectors and western designers. Crafted between 1870 and the mid 1930s, these unusual works were created by German or Scandinavian woodworkers who immigrated to the United States and bartered their work for food and lodging while traveling the country. These nomadic craftspeople layered Popsicle sticks or other small pieces of wood into unusual geometric shapes to create boxes, lamps, picture frames and small pieces of furniture. Often the work was ornamented with marbles, beads, bits of glass or pottery, brass tacks, and even little stones. Today Tramp Art is experiencing a revival, and prices range anywhere from $200 for a frame to $25,000 for a piece of furniture.

*T*hroughout her home, Robin Weiss has combined the cowboy look with Country style to create a feeling that is both comfortable and elegant. With Country furniture you can dress things up or down, she observes. By using willow furniture in the mix, Weiss captures a bit of Country sophistication. Her Vietnamese potbelly pig named Charlie trots around the kitchen and living area in his bandanna, oinking in approval of his surroundings.

*T*his needlepoint antique rocker, discovered by designer Astrid Sommer, can be a delicate touch in a masculine western room. ▲

◄ Designer Linda Bedell has created a cowboy ambiance by mixing old and new fabrics and textures in this young boy's room. The design includes drapes made of old cowboy blankets, an embossed leather chair with a sheepskin seat, and a vintage-fabric pillow. The Hudson Bay blanket on the bed complements the yippie-ei-o pattern on the bedding, copied from the original by Full Swing Company. Wrought-iron wall and floor lamps with rawhide-laced shades complete the classy cowpoke look.

*C*hoosing an interesting piece of furniture or decorative item is the key to Astrid Sommer's design philosophy. "I try to select pieces which have a distinct quality about them: a wonderful patina, a unique shape and interesting history," she says. She has spiced up the interior of her living room in Jackson Hole with a moose-antler footstool, Indian ceremonial masks on the wall, and a patina chest, which at one time was an old carriage seat. Through the large windows the mountain sunlight dances on the furniture, illuminating a composition which celebrates both nature and western culture. ◀ Photo © 1992 by David Swift, courtesy Astrid Sommer Interiors

▲ A Morris chair covered in pony hide stands next to a Stickley sideboard. The blue grass cloth walls and the iron candlesticks with the pony give this Craftsman look a rich and elegant cowpoke touch.

▶ A Molesworth chair highlights this eclectic western ski home. Couches draped with Indian blankets and adorned with pillows covered in Navajo blankets, a western fireplace screen and a cowhide rug complete this cozy living room. The fireplace is a Molesworth-inspired creation by Fighting Bear Antiques of Jackson Hole, Wyoming.

Photo © 1992 by David Swift, courtesy of The Great Bear Ranch

Photo © 1992 by David Swift, courtesy Astrid Sommer Interiors

A *pair of dangling spurs can be as effective in creating cowboy charm as a piece of western furniture.*

Photo © 1992 by Scott McKinley

JUST A TOUCH
OF COWBOY

Photo courtesy Tony Alvis

Cowboy silhouettes on a fireplace screen can discreetly bring the romantic West into any interior. Inspired by Molesworth silhouettes, Tony Alvis, a blacksmith and owner of Los Padres Wilderness Outfitters in southern California, creates works which look striking against a burning fire.

Whether decorating a room, an entire house or just a corner in the western style, sometimes less is more. Controlling the visual impact of the cowboy look is possible and at times desirable. A lodgepole couch may look strange in a chic New York studio apartment, but Fillerup's western drawer-pulls or Fighting Bear Enterprise's cowboy light switch plates can give a formal room some pizzazz and subtle humor. A unique lamp, a western pillow or a single cowboy chair can become a conversation piece, yet blend well in a variety of interiors.

Photo © 1992 by Sydney Gamble

Peter Fillerup's metal drawer pulls make this elegant bar, designed by Astrid Sommer, an elegant western display for Indian baskets. Fillerup casts each pull to give it texture and strength.

Photo © 1992 by Sydney Gamble

Cowboy light switch plates, designed by
Fighting Bear Enterprises, are a subtle way to
introduce the cowboy theme.

Old cowboy boots filled with pennies make
great bookends for favorite western novels.

Photo © 1992 by Scott McKinley

Photos © 1992 by Scott McKinley

Photo © 1992 by Scott McKinley

153

*T*he soft light from this floor lamp by True West Design in Clackamas, Oregon, washes a contemporary home with Old West romance.◀

▶ Jimmy Covert chose to incorporate bronze relief images by Peter Fillerup into his version of a western-style writing desk.

▼ A western oil painting by Charlie Dye and a few Indian motifs and Navajo rugs are just the touches that can soften the stern forms of the Craftsman style. Also note the cinches on the wall.

Photo courtesy of Elkhorn Design

Antler accessories date back to the 1600s in England, when huge antler chandeliers holding candles illuminated the dank castles and medieval homes. To keep this tradition alive, Richard Keene of Elkhorn Design in Jackson Hole, Wyoming, has maintained the rustic feeling in these antler pieces. Each of Richard Keene's antler chandeliers is a carefully balanced tribute to unrestricted wilderness.

Photo © 1992 by Scott Mckinley

*T*his wildlife sconce designed by Terry and Sandy Winchell of Fighting Bear Antiques conjures the romantic image of a moonlit night under the wide-open western sky.◀

▼ The buffalo wall sconce is handcrafted of old rusted iron and has a classic parchment-style shade. Designed by Mary Whitesides for the Sundance Catalog.

▶ This Mike Livingston chandelier would be a bright conversation piece in any room.

Photo © 1992, courtesy of Rituals

Photo courtesy Sundance Catalog

Quilts cut by Wolf Schlien and sewn by Lily Schlien make unique wall decorations. Almost all are one-of-a-kind. Visitors who stop by Quilts to Cover Your Fantasy, a chain in the West, can choose their own colors and designs for custom make-ups. Each quilt is sewn with a freehand guide, which allows the Schliens to produce shapes which are round or curved. Construction takes between ten and six hundred hours and quilts cost anywhere from $400–3,000.

The Schliens also design a pillow line which combines the look of hand appliqué with a blind stitch and appliquéd ultrasuede. Some pieces are outlined in fringe, while others have beaded tassels at the four corners.

Photo courtesy of Western Heritage Design

A sideboard like this one created by Western Heritage Designs is all you need to add to a room for a sophisticated and subtle western look.

*E*ntryways can be as fanciful and western as the inside of a home. Here, Jackson Hole resident Mike Jackson has carved a bear into the front door. ◀

▼ This boy's bedroom was created with the idea of making a cozy, functional and fun interior. Working with artist Carol Anne Haggerty, interior designer Astrid Sommer used paint to establish a whimsical western look amidst a collection of Arts and Crafts furniture and a Victorian bamboo chest. The walls were papered, then painted over with beige paint to produce a rugged textured look. To enrich the subtle hues of the walls and wood furniture, Sommer painted the picture molding with a brightly colored Indian pattern. The room features a pine sleigh bed with a brown faux inlay of Molesworth horses peering over a fence.

Photo © 1990 by John Vaughn

*T*he time period is right, so this funky Victorian chair, upholstered in suede, looks western against a background of cowboy and Indian memorabilia and a Navajo rug.

> *"With a touch of imagination and a brush, your straw rug can be a work of art and you can paint any design you want on it,"* Astrid Sommer says. In the long run the straw rug is less expensive than a Navajo or Ushak rug and still is a charming touch. *"The simpler a room the better,"* Sommer observes. *"In this case the Edward Grigware gunfighter design came to the rescue."*

Photo © 1992 by Emily A. Hart
Photo courtesy Cow Camp China

Western artist *Buckeye Blake* designed this china, which adds a funky modern flair to dishes and mugs. ▶

With contorted lodgepole, Bill Schenck designed and built his own bookcase, which stretches along the wall of his cabin and makes his cozy living room an ideal refuge for book lovers.

*C*owboy memorabilia, such as boots, hats, a rope and chaps, make interesting decorative items for a blank wall.

⬤SOURCES

Sleuthing the country for cowboy memorabilia and furniture can be a challenging experience as this mad dash for old cowboy items continues. But there are still plenty of small, out-of-the-way antique stores in the country where collectors might find old ropes, china, boots, rustic furniture, and branding irons languishing in a dark, dusty corner. Someone with a mind like Larry McMurtry's Cadillac Jack is bound to be rewarded. Never pass up a little store in the West with a sign that reads, "Groceries, Coffee, and Antiques." And city auctions and antique fairs like the one held each June in Teton Village, Wyoming, are also a must if you are on a cowboy treasure hunt.

Listed below, state by state, are some key design stores, furniture makers, and designers who can help you gather antique and contemporary pieces of furniture and accessories to create your dream home.

For Molesworth furniture, Fighting Bear Antiques of Jackson Hole, Wyoming, is still the best bet. Owners Sandy and Terry Winchell have probably seen and sold more Molesworth than anyone. They are passionate about Molesworth's work, striving to restore pieces as best they can to look like the originals, and they can tell you all about the history of the furniture.

FURNITURE MAKERS

Sam Bair
Route 4, Box 70 B
Santa Fe, New Mexico 87501
(505) 984-1301
Builds and designs lodgepole and rustic furniture.

Jim Barnaby
Neo Cowboy
P.O. Box 203
Bozeman, MT 59715
(406) 587-3585
Crafts western art-furniture. His work features bold color, shapes, and whimsical western characters.

L. D. Burke
Cowboy Furniture
1516 Pacheco St.
Santa Fe, New Mexico 87501

(505) 983-8001
Contemporary cowboy furniture maker and designer. Recognized in particular for his mirrors featuring cowboy sayings and decorated with spurs, rodeo belt buckles and other cowboy items.

Diane Cole
Rustic Furniture
10 Cloninger Lane
Bozeman, MT 59715
(406) 587-3373
Crafts classic willow and lodgepole furniture. Custom designs.

Indy Corson
Lupine Rustic Furniture
13750 Kelly Canyon Rd.

Bozeman, MT 59715
(406) 587-0672
Makes well-crafted lodgepole furniture. Often incorporates red-twig dogwood. Has worked with designer Hilary Heminway on custom designs.

Jimmy and Lynda Covert
907 Canyon Ave.
Cody, WY 82414
(307) 527-6761
Jimmy Covert creates some of the finest driftwood furniture in the West. He also builds Molesworth inspired pieces and reproductions. Lynda Covert designs leather pillows and does fine upholstery.

Harl Dixon
P.O. 17913

El Paso, TX 79917
(915) 858-5222
Sells antiques and makes custom cowboy and southwest furniture.

Jerry England
Lure of the Dim Trails
"Cowboy Chic" Pine Furniture
22647 Ventura Blvd., #358
Woodland Hills, CA 91364
(818) 702-0538
Builds custom furniture inspired by Molesworth's designs, sells western antiques, has designed his own fabric line and is a designer.

Roy Fisk
Fighting Bear Antiques
P.O. Box 3812
Jackson, WY 83001
Fighting Bear: (307) 733-2669
Creates one-of-a-kind western pieces, inspired by the Adirondack style. Limited production.

Larry Jansen
Lodgepole Furniture Manufacturer
Star Route Box 15
Jackson, WY 83001
(307) 733-3199
Complete line of rugged, handcrafted pole and rawhide furnishings for your home or business.

Mimi London
Mimi London, Inc.
Pacific Design Center, Suite G168
8687 Melrose Ave.
Los Angeles, CA 90069

(213) 855-2567
FAX (213) 855-0213
Has been designing her own lodgepole furniture since the seventies. Worked closely with well-known and respected designer Michael Taylor.

Randall Lovelady
Route 1
Box 826
Tuscola, TX 79562
(915) 554-7508
(915) 572-3638
Designs furniture and art pieces using horse shoes, wood and silhouettes.

Milo and Teddi Marks
Western Heritage Designs
P.O. Box 208
Hwy. 6
Meridian, TX 76665
(817) 435-2173
One of the few people to create high style long horn furniture. Also build fine pine furniture in the cowboy style.

Rob Mazza
Willow Run Woodworking
2330 Amsterdam Rd.
Belgrade, MT 59714
(406) 388-6848
Builds Molesworth-inspired furniture. He uses bright red leather, iron silhouettes on his furniture and designs his own cowboy lamps with rawhide shades.

Ron McGee's Wild West Furniture and Supply
P.O. Box 3010
Apache Junction, AZ 85220
(602) 983-1788
Designs solid and fun western pieces including furniture and accessories. Sells Navajo rugs, cowboy and Indian artifacts.

John Mortensen Studios
The Rainbow Trail Collection
1780 East 6400 South
Salt Lake City, UT 84121
(801) 278-4109
P.O. Box 746
Wilson, WY 83014
(307) 733-1519
Incorporates metal sculptured reliefs into furniture designs, lamps, and fireplace screens.

Mountain Breeze Inc. Lodgepole Furniture
857 Lincoln
P.O. Box 1672
Lander, WY 82520
(307) 332-2738
Design and build lodgepole furniture in the style of Molesworth.

National Upholstering Company
4000 Adeline St.
Oakland, CA 94608
(415) 653-8915
Offer a new western collection of handcrafted sofas and chairs, many upholstered in leather with hand-painted western designs.

Old Hickory Furniture Company, Inc.
403 South Noble St.
Shelbyville, IN 46176
(1-800) 232-BARK
FAX (317) 398-2275
Established in 1899. Built furniture for the Old Faithful Inn in Yellowstone. Now building cowboy furniture, covering hickory chairs with Pendleton blankets and hides, and continuing many of their traditional hickory designs.

Mike and Virginia Patrick
New West
Patrick Ranch
2119 Southfork
Cody, WY 82414
(307) 587-2839
Furniture makers and designers. They produce a large amount of furniture and were named top designers by Metropolitan Home in 1992.

Chuck Rowan
P.O. Box 669
Ranchos De Taos, NM 87557
(505) 758-4255
Designs western furniture with a touch of Santa Fe style.

Ken and Jill Siggins
Triangle Z Ranch Furniture
P.O. Box 995
Cody, WY 82414(307) 587-3901
Specialize in ranch lodgepole furniture. Also do custom work and restore Molesworth furniture.

Sweet Water Ranch
P.O. Drawer 398
Cody, WY 82414

(307) 527-4044 Shop
Sweet Water Ranch in Denver:
(303) 293-3171
Creates the finest Molesworth reproductions.

Bart and Mark Walker
P.O. Box 141
Victor, ID 83455
(208) 787-2851
Build fine custom lodgepole furniture.

DESIGNERS

AKM Interiors
Designer Anna Milner
1122 E. Main St., Suite #2
Bozeman, MT 59715
(406) 586-4261
Specialize in western design.

Salita Armour
Designer for John Williams Interiors
1859 West Lake Drive
Austin, TX 78746
(512) 328-2902
Recognized for her western interiors and work with L. D. Burke furniture. Designed rock star Jimmy Messina's home with Burke furniture.

Linda Bedell
Inner Design
P.O. Box 9305
Aspen, CO 81612

(303) 925-4310
FAX (303) 920-2615
High-end designer recognized for eclectic western interiors done for second homes.

Cabin Fever
Design Shop and Gifts
Robin Weiss
P.O. Box 1108
Jackson, WY 83001
(307) 733-0274
Designers Robin Weiss and Pamela Stockton. Their design showroom features a variety of cowboy accessories, gifts, and furniture.

Crybaby Ranch
Roxanne Thurmon and Judy Trattner
1422 Larimer
Denver, CO 80202
(303) 623-3979
Features cowboy mirrors and other work by Rick Montenerri. The design store also sells Molesworth and a fun mixture of contemporary and collectible western pieces.

Cynthia Hackett
Yippie-ei-o
1308 Montana Ave.
Santa Monica, CA 9040
(213) 451-2520
Qué Pasa
7051 5th Ave.
Scottsdale, AZ 85251
(602) 946-2918
Designers Cynthia Hackett and

Beth and Jim McClusky offer a variety of western furniture and accessories.

Hilary Heminway
243 Farmholm Rd.
Stonnington, CT 06378
(203) 535-3110
A designer who has been featured in publications such as HG for high-end ranch homes in the Rocky Mountain region.

Robert K. Lewis
Robert K. Lewis Associates, Inc., Interior Design
699 Madison Ave.
New York, NY 10021
(212) 755-1557
Lewis's work was featured in the June 1992 Wild West issue of Architectural Digest.

Raffia
Designer Linda Berman
10250 Santa Monica Blvd.
Los Angeles, CA 90067
(213) 201-0681
Features a stylish mix of old and new furniture and accessories. The store focuses on Americana and vintage western pieces.

The Ranch: Home Outfitters
Designer Linda Niven
601 E. Hopkins Ave.
Aspen, CO 81611
(303) 920-1079 W
Features a collection of western chic home furnishings, antiques, and their own line of accessories

such as pillows and lamps, inspired by traditional American Indian styles and materials.

Rituals
Marty Frenkel and Saundra Abbot, ASID
756 N. La Cienega Blvd.
Los Angeles, CA 90069
(310) 854-0848
Pioneers of the western look in an LA showroom. Features furniture, lighting, textiles, iron, and architectural elements, all in the western style as well as Arts and Crafts, Monterey, Mexican Ranch, Spanish Colonial, Southwest furniture and accessories. Exclusive showroom for Milo and Teddi Marks' furniture in Los Angeles

River Run Interiors
Mitch and LaVerne Thompson, ASID
105 North Broadway
Billings, MT 59101
(406) 256-0002
Does retail and interior design for residential and commercial clients. Specializes in regional design. Involved in a recent remodeling of the Old Faithful Inn.

Carol Sisson Design Associates
Jeanine Munro, Gail Kubik, Peggy Cole associates to Carol Sisson
117 E. Main
Bozeman, MT 59715
(406) 587-2600

Specialize in western design. Have used Rob Mazza furniture, accessories from The Ranch, and western fabrics such as Westgate.

Astrid Sommer Interiors
3742 Washington St.
San Francisco, CA 94118
(415) 751-5365
Accents ecclectic furniture combinations.

Charles Stuhlberg Gallery and Interior Design
511 E. Ave N.
Ketchum, ID 83340
(208) 726-4568
The gallery features a collection of furniture, antiques and accessories in the western style.

Harris Vanhee
P.O. Box 1126
Avon, CO 81620
(303) 949-1814
Designers Clair Vanhee and Meg Harris have done several projects using Molesworth and contemporary furniture.

Andrea Lawrence Wood Interior Design
1600 Wynkoop St., Suite 202
Denver, CO 80202
(303) 893-3263
100 W. Snow King Ave.
P.O. 20257
Jackson, WY 83001
(307) 733-1677
Specializes in high-end residential design throughout the western region. Recognized for rustic

western interiors. *Extensive resources for original pieces.*

Zoe's Best
330 E. Main St.
Aspen, CO 81611
(303) 925-6343
Sells antiques and contemporary western furniture and accessories, plus a variety of antler work and Indian artifacts.

RETAIL OUTLETS

Antēks
5812 W. Lovers Lane
Dallas, TX 75224
(214) 528-5567
Design a variety of western home furnishings. Their iron beds are particularly attractive. Also sell lodgepole bed frames.

Artifacts Gallery
308 E. Main St.
Bozeman, MT 59715
(406) 586-3755
American art and fine crafts, distinctive furniture and home accessories. Sells Rob Mazza furniture. Rustic style, contemporary.

Art Becker
Becker Gallery
102 Center St.
Jackson, WY 83001
(307) 733-1331
Specializes in antique Navajo rugs and blankets, Pueblo pottery, and Plains Indian beadwork.

Beyond Necessity Antiques and Folk Art
P.O. Box 271
Crabtree Corner
86 E. Broadway
Jackson, WY 83001
(307) 733-5634
Country antique furniture, rustic furniture and some western memorabilia.

Big Horn Gallery
1167 Sheridan Ave.
Cody, WY 82414
(307) 527-7587
On The Square
Jackson Hole, WY 83001
(307) 733-1434
Offers a fine collection of western art and features furniture makers Wally Reber, Ken Siggins, and Jimmy Covert.

Big Trails Western Antiques
John Christensen
709 Big Horn
Worland, WY 82401
(307) 347-3460
Sells mainly authentic cowboy memorabilia.

Buffalo Bill Museum
P.O. 1000, 720 Sheridan Ave.
Cody, WY 82414
(307) 587-4771
The museum features a permanent display of Molesworth furniture.

Butterfield Auctions
164 Utah St.
San Francisco, CA 94103

220 San Bruno Ave.
San Francisco, CA 94103
(415) 861-7500
Auctions always provide wonderful surprises and reasonable prices.

Cadillac Jack
Don Colclough
6911 Melrose
Los Angeles, CA 90038
(213) 931-8864
Large selection of vintage cowboy furniture and memorabilia including furniture from the 1930s–50s, lamps, boots, rodeo posters, and the largest selection of rodeo china. Restores pieces to a customer's preference.

Cowboy Coffee Shop
D. J. Appleman
P.O. Box 4
Big Sky, MT 59716
(406) 995-2618
A small coffee shop which sells cowboy coffee, western art and furniture.

Dakota
James and Cindy Gallusha
317 E. Colorado Ave.
Box 200
Telluride, CO 81435
(303) 728-4204 Dakota
Sells cowboy and country furnishings and accessories.

Alan Edison
American West Gallery
520 4th St.

Ketchum, ID 83340
(208) 726-1333
Offers vintage Pendleton and Beacon blankets, vintage Navajo weavings, period cowboy collectibles, Plains Indian beadwork, '40s and '50s cowboy collectibles, L. D. Burke furniture, western folk art, vintage Wild West posters, Molesworth furniture and vintage cowboy furniture.

Elkhorn Designs
Richard and Kathy Keene
P.O. Box 7663
70 S. Cache St.
Jackson, WY 83001
(307) 733-4655, phone and FAX
Features antler furniture and accessories including chandeliers, candlestick holders, fireplace sets, and sconces.

Elmer Diederich
(Old West Collectibles)
208 W. 6th
Big Timber, MT 59011
(406) 932-SPUR
Deals in serious cowboy collectibles, i.e., good-quality older western furniture, lamps and accessories. Shows by appointment only, or deals by mail.

Fighting Bear Antiques
Sandy and Terry Winchell
P.O. Box 3812
35 E. Simpson
Jackson, WY 83001
(307) 733-2669

Top dealer of Molesworth furniture and also sells Arts and Crafts, Country and Rustic pieces. Fighting Bear Enterprises also creates a limited amount of Molesworth-inspired iron work such as chandeliers, sconces, light switch plates, and fireplace screens.

Four Winds Indian Trading Post
Box 580
St. Ignatius, MT 59865
(406) 745-4336
A historic site in Montana which offers a large collection of Native American and frontier goods. Mimi London once noted this place for it's Native American carvings.

Furniture Etc.
Mary K. White
17 Main
Kalispell, MT 59901
(406) 756-8555
Features Molesworth furniture, lodgepole and willow furniture crafted locally, and antiques. The western showroom also sells a variety of cowboy and country accessories.

Galisteo
590 10th St.
San Francisco, CA 94103
(415) 861-5900
A cowboy and Santa Fe showroom featuring furniture and accessories.

Gene Autry Museum Shop
4700 Western Heritage Way
Los Angeles, CA 90027
(213) 667-2000
Sells Molesworth reproductions and a variety of cowboy accessories.

Homestead
Tim Bolton
223 E. Main
Fredericksburg, TX 78624
(512) 997-5551
Specializes in bedroom furniture and bed linens. Designs a wide variety of cowboy pieces ranging from horseshoe furniture to carved cowboy beds and curtain rods. Will ship anywhere.

Martin-Harris Gallery
Martin and Jan Kruzich
Ronald and Joan Harris
60 East Broadway, Suites 3-5
upstairs
Box 2968
Jackson, WY 83001
(800) 366-7841
(307) 733-0350
The gallery sells fine art and furniture of the new West, including Rob Mazza's. They also sell old saddles, spurs and other cowboy and Indian memorabilia.

Mountain House
P.O. Box 435
140 East Broadway
Jackson, WY 83001
(307) 733-4227

A middle to high-end home furnishing store specializing in western decor. Has a large collection of furniture and accessories, including antler and some iron work. Sells furniture by John Mortensen and Ron McGee.

The Naturalist
1080 S. 350 E.
Provo, UT 84603
(800) 344-7244
Specializes in rustic American frontier style furniture and decorative items, including pillows, bedcovers, throws and some ironwork. Carries Mary Whitesides' line. Sells worldwide.

Old Taos
108 Teresina Lane
Taos, NM 87571
(505) 758-7353
Specializes in cowboy gear and Native American handiwork.

One Eyed Jack's
1645 Market St.
San Francisco, CA 94103
(415) 621-4390
Specializes in American country and western furniture, western collectibles, rugs, boots, and bones.

Osprey Nest Antiques
Karen Nagelhus
Box 300
Hwy. 93 South
Somers, MT 59932

(406) 857-3714
Sells a collection of furniture from country to English. Also cowboy memorabilia, and old creels, snowshoes, and skis.

D. J. Puffert
The Arts and Crafts Shop
1417 Bridgeway
Sausalito, CA 94965
(415) 331-2554
Offers a comprehensive collection of Arts and Crafts furnishings. The shop features pottery, copper, lighting, paintings, furniture, and textiles.

Rainbow Man
Bob and Marianne Kapoun
107 E. Palace Ave.
Santa Fe, NM 87501
(505) 982-8706
Considered leading authorities on Indian trade blankets. Sells other trade blankets including 1920 Pendeltons; also sells '40s and '50s cowboy and Indian memorabilia, and have the largest retail collection of Edward Curtis vintage photographs.

Ralph Lauren Home Collection
1185 Ave. of the Americas
New York, NY 10036
(212) 642-8700 (for the store nearest you)

Santa Fe
3571 Sacramento St.
San Francisco, CA 94118
(415) 346-0180

The finest in authentic old Southwest furniture, western art, Navajo goods, and cowboy relics and memorabilia. A good place to find Borein etchings, old ranch tables, and turquoise and silver jewelry.

Shaboom's
Jackie Stufflebeam
5811 N. Seventh St.
Phoenix, AZ 85014
(602) 222-5432
Specializes in vintage cowboy furniture, accessories, fabrics, boots and old Levi's advertisements. Also has wagon wheel and ranch oak furniture and Roy Rogers, Hopalong Cassidy and Gene Autry memorabilia.

Showcase Antiques
James L. Putman
115 E. Broadway
Jackson, WY 83001
(307) 733-7133
Specialize in authentic Early American art, antiques, Amish quilts, and unusual collectibles.

Silverland
7066 Fifth Ave.
Scottsdale, AZ 85251
(602) 947-8569
For collectors searching for new Navajo rugs, traditional and contemporary Indian jewelry and other Hopi, Zuni and Navajo arts and crafts, Silverland is a good place to start.

Jane Smith
201 S. Galena
Aspen, CO 81611
(303) 925-6105
A western fashion boutique which features furniture by L. D. Burke.

T and A Antiques
155 W. Pearl Ave.
Jackson, WY 83001
(307) 733-9717
A collection of furniture, accessories, and jewelry from the 1920s–50s. One may also find funky cowboy lamps, knickknacks, saddle purses and some vintage western clothing.

ACCESSORIES

Tony Alvis
Los Padres Wilderness Outfitters
6855 Vista Del Rincon
Ventura, CA 93001
(805) 648-2113
A blacksmith and outfitter who crafts fine metalwork such as fireplace screens, tables, gates and signs featuring western silhouettes.

The Bayley Bonnet Company
311 Old La Honda Rd.
Woodside, CA 94062
(415) 851-2696
Sells fashionable bonnets for all seasons. Bonnets are made of the finest chintz lace, corduroy, and velvet.

Tyler and Teresa Beard
True West
Box 48
802 South Austin St.
Comanche, TX 76442
(915) 356-2140
The Beards sell reproductions of Wallace China. They are also buyers of western furniture and memorabilia.

Janet Bedford
858 Lane 4
Powell, WY 82435
(307) 754-3067
A freelance artist who designs original cowboy lamp bases and painted parchment shades.

John Bickner
P.O. Box 129
Teton Village, WY 83025
(307) 733-3916
Designs antler chandeliers and other antler accessories.

Steve Blood
P.O. 295
Boston, NY 14025
(716) 941-6841
Crafts cowboy cutout lamps in the tradition of his father Russell Blood, a former Molesworth employee.

Cow Camp China
6 Onion Blvd.
Shrewsbury, PA 17361
(717) 235-8998

Sells the Buckeye Blake china pattern.

Bill Feeley
P.O. Box 2245
Cody, WY 82414
(307) 587-5194
Designs iron chandeliers, sconces, and fireplace screens in the Molesworth style. Incorporates wrought-iron silhouette images of wildlife and cowboy into his work.

Peter and Lisa Fillerup
P.O. Box 286
Heber, UT 84032
(801) 654-4151
Peter Fillerup designs chandeliers and sconces using relief figures. He also designs decorative drawer pulls and bronze relief images for furniture.

Flat Creek Saddle Shop
265 W. Broadway
P.O. Box 2069
Jackson, WY 83001
(307) 733-1260
Custom leather work by Scott Carter and Chris Blandi.

Norman Foss
Leonard Foss Studios
1340 E. 12th St.
Oakland, CA 94606
(800) 237-4233
Have been making stretched rawhide lamp shades since 1919. They were one of Molesworth's suppliers and still prosper today.

Galeria San Ysidro
Box 17913
El Paso, TX 79917
(915) 858-5222
Complete line of ironwork,
including lamps, andirons, candle
holders, and pot stands.

Chris and Gary Gallusha
5 Baya Court
Santa Fe, NM 87505
(505) 986-0718
Create a variety of leather
products including lamp shades,
leather boxes and frames.

Sharon and Larry Hitchcock
True West Design
21800 Hwy. 224 SE
Clackamas, OR 97015
(503) 658-8753
Design fun functional art for
homes. They do a variety of
wrought-iron sconces and lamps
featuring cowboy images.

Peter Houghtaling
Custom Textiles
P.O. Box 160365
Austin, TX 78716-0365
(512) 327-4207
Creates custom textiles including
Navajo reproductions.

Bill Schenck
Moran, WY 83013
(307) 543-2302 summer
144 South 85th St.
Mesa, AZ 85208
(602) 986-7028 winter
(602) 982-4105 winter

Schenck is a western pop artist
and sells Native American pottery.

Wolf and Lily Schlien
Textile Communications
P.O. Box 246
Glorieta, NM 87535
(505) 757-6689
Design custom cowboy quilts,
wall hangings and pillows.

Jackson Signs
Mike Jackson
1084 U.S. Hwy. 89
P.O. Box 7016
Jackson, WY 83001
(307) 733-7755
Specializes in hand carved
western signs, doors and ranch
gates.

Taos Drum
South Santa Fe Rd., south of Taos
P.O. Box 1916
Taos, NM 87591
(505) 758-3796
(800) 424-DRUM
Makes Native American drums
and crafts furniture and
accessories from drums. Also
makes wooden lamp frames and
rawhide lamp shades.

Mike Wilson
Big Horn Antler Furniture and
Design
P.O. Box 306
Jackson, WY 83001
(307) 733-3491
Designs and builds some of the
finest antler furniture and
accessories in Wyoming.